PLAY GAMES WITH ENGLISH

1

TEACHER'S RESOURCE BOOK

COLIN GRANGER
with illustrations by John Plumb

Revised edition in 3 levels

Heinemann Games Series

Titles in this series include:

Play Games With English Teacher's Resource Book 1 Colin Granger 0 435 25016 7
Play Games With English Teacher's Resource Book 2 Colin Granger 0 435 25017 5

Word Games with English 1 Deirdre Howard-Williams & Cynthia Herd 0 435 28380 4
Word Games with English 2 Deirdre Howard-Williams & Cynthia Herd 0 435 28381 2
Word Games with English 3 Deirdre Howard-Williams & Cynthia Herd 0 435 28382 0
Word Games with English Plus Deirdre Howard-Williams & Cynthia Herd 0 435 28379 0

English Puzzles 1 Doug Case 0 435 28280 8
English Puzzles 2 Doug Case 0 435 28281 6
English Puzzles 3 Doug Case 0 435 28282 4
English Puzzles 4 Doug Case 0 435 28283 2

Heinemann International
a division of Heinemann Publishers (Oxford) Ltd
Halley Court, Jordan Hill, Oxford OX2 8EJ

OXFORD LONDON EDINBURGH MADRID ATHENS BOLOGNA
MELBOURNE SYDNEY AUCKLAND IBADAN NAIROBI GABORONE HARARE
KINGSTON PORTSMOUTH (NH) SINGAPORE

ISBN 0 435 25016 7

Acknowledgements

We would like to thank David King of the Davies School of English in Brighton for his help in the preparation of this book. Also to teachers at the LTC School of English, London and the Migros Klubschule, Basle. Finally to Jathan and Nicola for ideas and suggestions for language games.

© Colin Granger and John Plumb 1993
First published 1993

Cover designed by Martin Cox
Illustrations and student's pages designed by John Plumb
Teacher's pages typeset by The Design Syndicate

Printed in Great Britain by Thomson Litho Ltd, Scotland

93 94 95 96 97 10 9 8 7 6 5 4 3 2 1

CONTENTS

Contents continued ...

TEACHER'S INTRODUCTION

In **Play Games With English 1** you will find **43 main games** on the photocopiable students' pages of the book and a further **50 follow-up games** outlined on the accompanying teacher's pages. Please note that you need to photocopy 2 pages for some of the **Memory** games. On pages where you see a hand with a pen symbol ✏️ ask the students to write the answers in their exercise books.

Play Games With English 1 can be used in two ways:

- *systematically* Playing each main game in turn with as many of the follow up games as you think necessary. As the games are graded, you will be providing systematic practice of language structures appropriate to students at a beginner or false beginner level. The **Contents** on page 3 will show you what language points each game practises.

- *selectively* Choosing and playing games to provide additional practice of points you feel your students need extra help with. The **Index of Structure and Language Points** on page 96 will help you to select games to fit your students' needs.

USING LANGUAGE GAMES IN THE CLASSROOM

Most games in **Play Games With English 1** have four stages:

1. *The Rules of the Game*
    Generally, the best way of getting the students to understand how a game is played is not to explain the rules but to play a trial round with the students.

2. *Choosing Sides*
    The games in **Play Games With English 1** can be played in the following ways:

    • *Player A v.Player B* Here each person in the class plays against each other.
    • *Small team v. Small team* Here the class is divided up into a number of small teams .
    • *Team A v. Team B* Here the class is divided into two teams.
    • *You v. the class* Here you (or individual students in turn) play against the rest of the class.
    Some games are best played in one particular way; in others you can be more flexible. If the students organise themselves into teams, make sure that not all the best students end up in the same team.

3. *Playing the Game*
    In games involving team discussion, stress to your students that the working language should, as far as possible, be English.

    Correction
    While the game is being played, any correction of mistakes should be done in as unobtrusive a way as possible so as not to distract from the game.

4. *Follow up*
    The purpose of this stage is to focus the students' attention on the main language points practised in the game. At this stage, any mistakes made during the game can be corrected and any new vocabulary written up.

MEMORY 1

Articles *(a, an)*: *a pie, an orange*
Cardinal Numbers + Plural Nouns: *six eggs*

Divide the class into small teams of two to three players and appoint team secretaries. Give the teams two minutes to study the picture and then ask them to cover the picture so it cannot be seen. The team secretaries, helped by the other players in their team, then have to write down as many objects as they can remember. Make sure they write either an article or a number before each object, e.g. *an apple, seven tomatoes*. Set a time limit of five minutes for this task. The team with the most correct answers is the winner.

ANSWERS:			
	an apple	seven tomatoes	a pie
	six eggs	an orange	eight biscuits
	four sandwiches	two bananas	five cakes
	four lemons	a cabbage	five potatoes
	nine sweets	two pears	three onions

THE LONG SENTENCE GAME

***Have got* + Articles *(a, an)*:** *I've got a cake.*
Cardinal Numbers + Plural Nouns: *I've got six pens.*

Begin the game by saying *I've got a cake.* Explain that the first player has to repeat this sentence and add a new object or objects, e.g. *I've got a cake and two pens.* The game continues with each player in turn trying to remember what the last player said, and then adding on a new item to the sentence. Players get minus points if they *(a)* make a memory mistake; or *(b)* hesitate too long. Do not give players minus points for grammar mistakes – just correct the mistake and let the player continue.
Example round with a group of five players:

Player 1:	*I've got a cake and two pens.*
Player 2:	*I've got a cake, two pens and a book.*
Player 3:	*I've got a cake, two pens, a book and six keys.*
Player 4:	*I've got a cake, a book …*
	(This player makes a memory mistake and so gets a minus point.)
Player 5:	*I've got a cake, two pens, a book, six keys and an apple.*
Player 1:	*I've got a cake, two pens, … etc.*

And so on. You could then begin a new game with a different basic sentence, e.g. *He's got a car …*The player with the least number of minus points at the end of the game is the winner.
Hints: Play a trial round before playing properly.

BUZZ

Cardinal Numbers: *one, two,* etc.

The first player calls out *one*, the next player *two,* the next *three*, and so on, around the class. As soon as the number *five* or any multiple thereof (10, 15, 20, 25, etc.) is reached, the player whose turn it is must say *buzz*. If the number contains a five but is not a multiple of five, only part of it is replaced by buzz, e.g. *54* would be *buzz-four*.
Players get minus points if they *(a)* forget to say *buzz*; or *(b)* hesitate too long. The player with the least number of minus points at the end of the game is the winner.

FIZZ

Fizz is played exactly like **Buzz**, except the players say *fizz* for sevens or multiples of seven.

1. Look at the picture for two minutes.

2. Cover the picture.

3. Write down all the things you can remember.

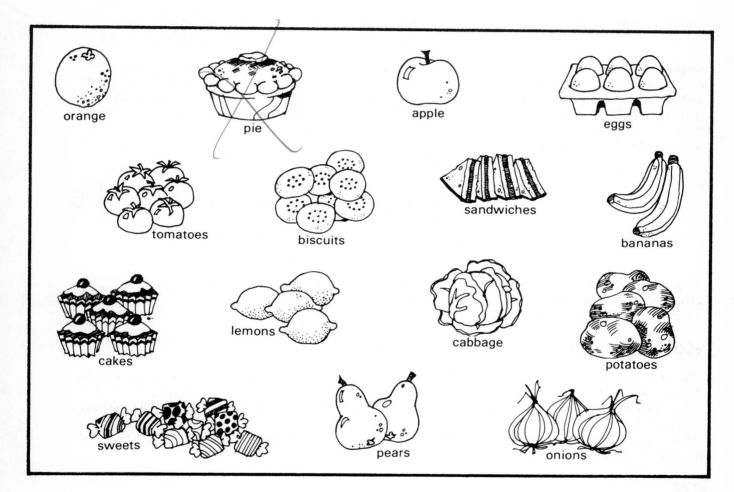

orange   pie   apple   eggs

tomatoes   biscuits   sandwiches   bananas

cakes   lemons   cabbage   potatoes

sweets   pears   onions

an apple, seven tomatoes, a pie...

7

THE NAME GAME

Personal Pronouns + Verb *to be*: *It's a telephone.*
They're books.
This/These: *What's this? What are these?*

Divide the class into two teams (Team A and Team B). The two teams take it in turns to ask the other team *What's this?* and *What are these?* questions about the picture. For example:

Team A:	(about object 3): *What's this?*
Team B:	*It's an alarm-clock.*
Team B:	(about object 4): *What's this?*
Team A:	*It's a light.*

The players in each team should take it in turns to ask and answer questions. Score 1 point per correct question, 2 points per correct answer. The team with the most points at the end is the winner.

ANSWERS:			
1.	It's a telephone.	8.	It's a pillow.
2.	They're books.	9.	It's a heater.
3.	It's an alarm clock.	10.	It's an armchair.
4.	It's a table lamp/a light.	11.	It's a rug/mat.
5.	It's a stereo system/ compact disc/CD player.	12.	It's a towel.
		13.	It's a window.
6.	It's a tap.	14.	It's a toothbrush.
7.	They're blankets.	15.	It's a mirror.

THE NAME GAME – extension

This/That/These/Those: *What's that? What are those?*
Personal Pronouns + Verb *to be*: *It's a window.*

Continue as above but this time with questions about objects in the room.
Introduce the use of *this* and *these* for **near** and *that* and *those* for **far** singular and plural objects, by providing some example questions before playing the game.
Hints: You could make the vocabulary more interesting and varied by getting the players to place personal possessions in view.

THE NAME GAME

How many things can you name?

1. *It's a telephone.*
2. *They're books.*
3. ....
4. ....
5. ....
6. ....
7. ....
8. ....

9. ....
10. ....
11. ....
12. ....
13. ....
14. ....
15. ....

SHADOWS

Personal Pronouns + Verb *to be* *He's a dentist.*
They're footballers.

Divide the class into small teams of two to three players. Appoint team secretaries. Set a time limit of five minutes for the team secretaries, helped by the rest of their team, to write down what the various jobs are. The team with the most correct sentences is the winner.

ANSWERS:	1. He's a dentist.	6.	She's a nurse.
	2. They're footballers.	7.	He's a chef.
	3. He's a gardener.	8.	He's a window cleaner.
	4. She's a teacher.	9.	They're waitresses.
	5. They're decorators.	10.	They're secretaries.

WHAT'S MY JOB?

Verb *to be* + Personal Pronouns: *Are you a doctor?*
Yes, I am./No, I'm not.

Ask one of the players to write the name of a job on a slip of paper and hand it to you, without any of the other players seeing it. Mime an action which is associated with the job. Your mime does not have to be good, in fact it is better if you do not mime the job too clearly as this makes it too easy to guess what the job is. Then get the rest of the players to try to guess your job: *Are you a doctor? Are you a butcher?* Answer with *Yes, I am* or *No, I'm not.* Give further mime or verbal hints if the class find it impossible to guess, e.g. if you are a car mechanic say *garage.* You can also guide the class to the right answer by saying a definite *no* if they are way off the mark, and an encouraging *no* if they are getting warm. The player who guesses the right answer gets the chance to mime the next job for the others to guess, and so on, until everyone has had a turn.

Hints: Practise *Is he/Is she* questions by getting two players to think of a job; one then mimes an action associated with the job while the other answers the questions.

Encourage interesting jobs by suggesting jobs for the students to take on, e.g. *a window cleaner, a spy, a surgeon, an optician, an undertaker, a football referee, a farmer, a scientist.*

SHADOWS

What are their jobs?

Use these words:

dentist   waitress   secretary   footballer   decorator

window cleaner   nurse   chef   teacher   gardener

1. He's a dentist.

2. They're footballers.

3. ....

4. ....

5. ....

6. ....

7. ....

8. ....

9. ....

10. ....

MIME GAME

Present Continuous: *He's shaving.*

Divide the class into small teams of two to three players and appoint team secretaries. Set a time limit of five to eight minutes for the team secretaries, helped by the rest of their team, to write down the actions being mimed in the pictures. The team with the most correct sentences is the winner.

Hints: Point out the spelling rule SHAVE + ING = SHAVING before playing the game.

ANSWERS:		
	1. He's shaving.	5. She's combing her hair.
	2. She's playing the piano.	6. She's drinking a cup of tea.
	3. He's cleaning his teeth.	7. He's driving.
	4. He's going upstairs.	8. She's telephoning.

MIME GAME – extension

Present Continuous: *Are you combing your hair?*
Yes, I am./No, I'm not.

Ask one of the players to write an action on a slip of paper and hand it to you, without any of the other players seeing it. Mime the action for the rest of the group to guess: *Are you combing your hair? Are you brushing your hair?* Answer with *Yes, I am* or *No, I'm not.* (Your mime does not have to be good — the more amateur the mime, the more questions will have to be asked.) Give verbal hints if necessary. The player who guesses the right answer then gets the chance to mime an action for the others to guess, and so on, until everyone has had a turn.

Hints: You could practise *Is he/Is she* questions by getting two students to think of an action; one then mimes the action while the other answers the questions. If the players cannot think of an action to mime, you could suggest *washing hands, telephoning, driving a car, playing chess, lighting a fire, making an omelette, having a shower.* Another variant of the game is to suggest different categories such as *eating something, cooking something, doing something in the house, playing a game.* Each player then has to mime, for example, eating a different kind of food for the others to guess, e.g. *eating spaghetti, eating an egg, eating peas.*

MIME GAME

What are these people doing?

Use these words:

shave   comb her hair   drive a car   drink a cup of tea   play the piano

clean his teeth   go upstairs   phone

1. *He's shaving.*

2. ....

3. ....

4. ....

5. ....

6. ....

7. ....

8. ....

13

OPPOSITES QUIZ

Adjectives: *happy/sad*

Divide the class into small teams of two to three players and appoint team secretaries. Set a time limit of three to five minutes for the team secretaries, helped by the rest of their team, to write the opposites. The team with the most correct opposites is the winner.

ANSWERS:				
	1.	happy/sad	7.	young/old
	2.	good/bad	8.	wrong/right
	3.	poor/rich	9.	strong/weak
	4.	small/big	10.	heavy/light
	5.	ill/well	11.	cold/hot
	6.	old/new	12.	short/tall

ADJECTIVES GAME

Have got + Adjective + Noun: *He's got a blue car.*

Write up the basic structure *He's got a/an ... car*. Begin the game by saying *He's got a blue car*. Explain that each player in turn has to say the same sentence but with a different adjective, for example:

Player 1:	*He's got an old car.*
Player 2:	*He's got a fast car.*
Player 3:	*He's got a comfortable car.*

Players get minus points if they (*a*) are unable to think of a new adjective; (*b*) repeat an adjective which has been previously used; (*c*) use an inappropriate adjective; or (*d*) hesitate too long.
Example round with a group of five players:

Player 1:	*He's got an old car.*
Player 2:	*He's got a fast car.*
Player 3:	*He's got a comfortable car.*
Player 4:	*He's got ...*
	(This player hesitates too long and so gets a minus point.)
Player 5:	*He's got a slow car.*
Player 1:	*He's got a new car.*

And so on. Start a new round of the game with a different base sentence and a different vocabulary area as soon as players begin to run out of ideas.
The player with the least number of minus points at the end of the game is the winner.
Hints: Suggestions for further games: *They've got a/an ... house; We've got a/an ... dog; She's got a/an ... coat; I've got a/an ... book.*

OPPOSITES QUIZ

Find the opposite to these words.

1. HAPPY
2. GOOD
3. POOR
4. SMALL
5. ILL
6. OLD
7. YOUNG
8. WRONG
9. STRONG
10. HEAVY
11. COLD
12. SHORT

HOT · SAD · WELL · LIGHT · BIG · NEW · WEAK · RICH · TALL · BAD · OLD · RIGHT

1. Happy / Sad
2. ....
3. ....
4. ....
5. ....
6. ....
7. ....
8. ....
9. ....
10. ....
11. ....
12. ....

15

VERB GAME

Present Continuous: *I'm watching television in the living room.*

Working individually (or in pairs), the players have to write down as many sentences as they can in the five minute time limit. The player with the most correct sentences is the winner.

ANSWERS:	1. I'm watching television in the living room.	7. They're cleaning their teeth in the bathroom.
	2. She's having a shower in the bathroom.	8. I'm listening to music in the living room.
	3. We're eating sandwiches in the kitchen.	9. They're putting on their clothes in the bedroom.
	4. She's writing a letter in the living room.	10. We're playing table tennis in the bedroom.
	5. We're making tea in the kitchen.	11. He's washing the dishes in the kitchen.
	6. He's reading a book in living room.	

THE HIDDEN PICTURE GAME

Present Continuous: *Is he eating an apple?*
Yes, he is./No, he isn't.

Draw a simple sketch of someone doing something. Do not let anyone see what you are drawing. The class then has to try to guess what the person you have drawn is doing.
Answer with short answers, e.g.

Is he reading?	*No, he isn't.*
Is he eating something?	*No, he isn't.*
Is he making something?	*Yes, he is.*
Is he making the bed?	*Yes, he is.*

Continue the game either by getting the player who guessed correctly to draw someone doing something for the others to guess, or by drawing the sketches yourself and giving them to different players to use.
Hints: Some suggested drawings:

Practise the *they* form with pictures showing two people doing the same action, e.g.

Alternatively, you could use pictures cut out from magazines.

16

VERB GAME

 1. Choose a picture.   2. Find the room.

Use these verbs:						
watch	make	clean	eat	listen to	write	play	have	put on	wash up	read

1. *I'm watching television in the living room.*
2. ....
3. ....
4. ....
5. ....
6. ....
7. ....
8. ....
9. ....
10. ....
11. ....

17

Present Simple: *She drives a car.*

three players and appoint team secretaries. Give the teams ten
for the team secretaries, helped by the rest of the players in
ut Nicola. The team with the most correct sentences is the

int out the evidence for their statements, e.g. *She plays the*
cord player.

ANSWERS:		
	She plays the guitar.	She drinks coffee.
	She listens to classical music.	She eats spaghetti.
	She reads magazines.	She watches television/TV.
	She wears jeans.	She takes photographs/photos.

OBSERVATION 1 – extension

Present Simple: *You eat sweets.*

Ask the class to empty out the contents of their pockets, handbags, briefcases, etc. The class then has to deduce things about each player in turn, e.g.

You eat sweets.   (a packet of sweets)
You travel by bus.   (an old bus ticket)

Hints: You will probably manage to persuade everyone to reveal their personal possessions if you start off with your own things. If this does prove to be a problem, bring in a number of objects and assign them to fictitious characters.

OBSERVATION 1

This is Nicola.
Nicola is a student.

This is her room.

You don't know Nicola,
but you can write a
lot about her just by
looking at her room.
For example:

 She drives a car.   She studies science.

Write eight more sentences about Nicola.

Use these verbs:							
play	listen to	read	wear	drink	eat	watch	take

1. ....

2. ....

3. ....

4. ....

5. ....

6. ....

7. ....

8. ....

MEMORY 2

There is/There are: *There's a shirt.*
There are two pairs of shoes.
Some: *There are some magazines.*

Divide the class into small teams of two to three players and appoint team secretaries. Give the teams two minutes to study the picture and then ask them to cover the picture so it cannot be seen. The team secretaries, helped by the other players in their team, then have to write down what is in the suitcase. They must not look at the picture while doing this. Each team then reads out their list of sentences. The team with the most correct sentences is the winner. Alternatively, score two points if the sentences are **both** grammatically and factually correct, one point if only factually correct. The team with the most points is the winner.

ANSWERS:		
	There are two pairs of shoes.	There's a shirt.
	There are some magazines.	There's a pullover.
	There are some socks.	There's a pair of trousers.
	There are two pairs of sunglasses.	There's a book.
	There are some handkerchiefs.	There's a brush.
	There's a comb.	There's a toothbrush.
	There are three ties.	There's a towel.

MEMORY 2 – extension

There is/There are + a/any: *Is there a book/any milk on the table? Yes, there is./No, there isn't.*
Are there any matches on the table?
Yes, there are./No, there aren't.

Place a large number of objects on a table or desk. For example: *paper, magazines, a book, bread, a newspaper, matches, a ring, an empty cup, sugar, some files, a cassette.* It would be better if you could do this without the class seeing you. Allow the class one minute to study what is on the table. Then cover the objects. Then ask the class questions about what is on the table. Take care to ask questions which require a negative as well as a positive answer. For example:

Is there a glass on the table?	*No, there isn't.*
Is there a cup on the table?	*Yes, there is.*
Are there any files on the table?	*Yes, there are.*
Is there any tea on the table?	*No, there isn't.*

Allow the class a few moments for consultation before they answer. Write their answers up in note form, e.g. *glass/no; cup/yes,* etc. Then uncover the objects and award 1 point for each correct answer.
Then get the class to test your memory. Play as above, but this time you have to answer the players' *Is there/Are there* questions.

1. Look at this picture for two minutes.

2. Cover the picture.

3. Write down all the things you can remember.

What's in the suitcase?

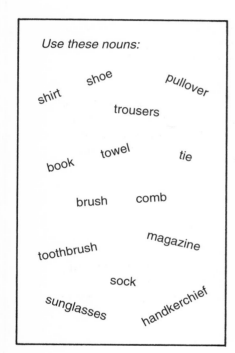

Use these nouns:

shirt shoe pullover trousers book towel tie brush comb toothbrush magazine sock sunglasses handkerchief

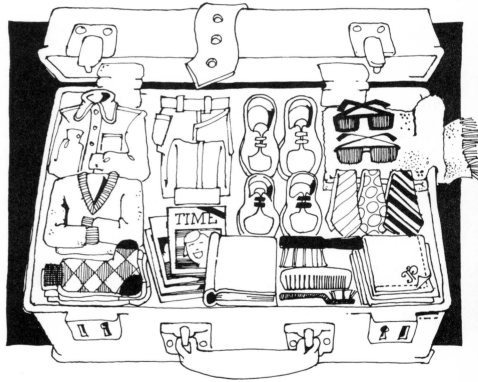

There's a shirt, there are two pairs of shoes, there are some magazines.

....

....

....

....

....

....

21

JOBS QUIZ

Present Simple: *She answers the telephone.*

Working individually (or in pairs), the players write down two sentences for each character. Set a ten to fifteen- minute time limit. The player with the most correct sentences is the winner.

ANSWERS:		
	1. Sally answers the telephone.	She types letters.
	2. Kate writes on the blackboard.	She marks homework.
	3. Jason gives change.	He serves customers.
	4. Steve wallpapers rooms.	He paints doors.
	5. Bob cuts the grass.	He waters the flowers.
	6. Carol takes photographs.	She develops films.

20 QUESTIONS – JOBS

Present Simple: *Do you work outside?*
Yes, I do./No, I don't.
Does he work in an office?
Yes, he does./No, he doesn't.

Introduce some useful vocabulary for this game by discussing your own job, for example:

What's my job?	*You're a teacher.*
What do I teach?	*You teach English.*
Where do I work?	*You work in a school.*
Who do I work for?	*You work for …*
Do I work inside or outside?	*You work inside.*
Do I wear special clothes for my job?	*No, you don't.*

Write the name of a job on a slip of paper, and assign it to a fictitious friend. The class has to guess the job by asking *Does* questions, for example:

Does he work outside?	*No, he doesn't.*
Does he earn a lot of money?	*Yes, he does.*

Divide the class into two teams (Team A and Team B). The two teams take it in turns to write down the name of a job for the other team to guess. Each team has 20 questions with which to find out the job. Write up the score, like this: e.g. If Team B gets the answer in fourteen questions, write: *Team B 14.* If Team B fails to guess the job in twenty questions, write: *Team B 20.* At the end, the team with the **lowest** total is the winner.

Hints: Suggest that the teams allocate each job to a particular member of the team; in this way, various forms can be practised, e.g.:

Does she drive a bus?
Do you work with children?

Encourage the teams to choose unusual jobs (*bullfighter, astronaut, gangster, nun, clown,* etc.) rather than ordinary jobs.

JOBS QUIZ

1. Sally
a secretary

2. Kate
a teacher

3. Jason
a shop assistant

4. Steve
a decorator

5. Bob
a gardener

6. Carol
a photographer

Find two things that these people do in their jobs.

telephone   blackboard   grass   letters

film   change   customers   photographs

rooms   doors   homework   flowers

Use these verbs: water   type   give   develop   wallpaper

answer   write on   cut   mark   take   paint   serve

1. Sally answers the telephone.
   She types letters.

2.

3.

4.

5.

6.

23

WHERE?

Working individually (or in pairs), the players write down as many sentences as they can in the five minute time limit. The player with the most correct sentences is the winner.

Hints: Alternatively, you could play this as a speed game, telling the players that there are sixteen mice which they have to locate in the picture. The first player to write the sixteen sentences correctly is the winner.

ANSWERS:	There's a mouse:	
	in the cupboard.	behind the sink.
	behind the door.	in front of the salt.
	in the oven.	on the chair.
	on top of the cupboard.	under the chair.
	in the saucepan.	on top of the piece of cheese.
	in the sink.	in the cup.
	in the drawer.	between the glass and the cup.
	in front of the cat.	on the plate.

HIDE AND SEEK

Prepositions of Place: *Is the ring on something?*
Yes, it is./No, it isn't.

You need two small objects for this game, for example, *a ring* and *a pair of scissors*. It is important that one of these objects should be something that requires the plural, e.g. *scissors, spectacles*. Leave the room for a short time, telling the class to hide the two objects in two separate places while you are gone. Come back into the room and first ask questions to find out where the ring is hidden, e.g.

Is the ring on something?	*No, it isn't.*
Is it under something?	*No, it isn't.*
Is it behind something?	*Yes, it is.*
Is it behind the curtains?	*No, it isn't.*

When you have found the ring try to locate the scissors:

Are the scissors in something? etc.

Then the players can take over the guessing role by leaving the room for a moment while the objects are hidden in new places. To score this game, count the number of questions each player requires before finding the objects. The player with the **lowest** number is the winner.

Hints: With a large class, speed up the game by sending more than one player out of the room at a time, and having them ask questions in turn. If you want to avoid sending players out of the room, imaginary hiding places could be written down.

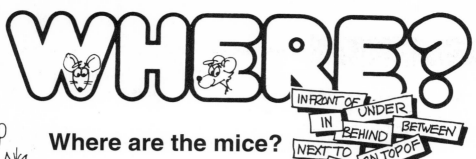

WHERE?

Where are the mice?

IN FRONT OF UNDER
IN BEHIND BETWEEN
NEXT TO ON TOP OF
ON

You have five minutes to find them.
There are sixteen mice.

Use these words:						
		cupboard	sink	drawer	glass	cup	saucepan
oven	door		salt	plate	cat	chair	piece of cheese

There's a mouse in the cupboard.

....

There's a mouse behind the door.

....

....

....

....

....

....

....

....

SPELLING PUZZLE

Spelling; Vocabulary

Working individually (or in pairs), the players write down the correct spelling of the different objects. The player who does this in the shortest time is the winner.

ANSWERS:						
	1.	bottle	7.	fifty	13.	saucepan
	2.	curtains	8.	queue	14.	lorry
	3.	knives	9.	sixteen	15.	beach
	4.	magazines	10.	biscuits		
	5.	shower	11.	blankets		
	6.	pyjamas	12.	dining room		

HANGMAN

Alphabet; Spelling; Vocabulary

Divide the class into two teams (Team A and Team B) and appoint team secretaries. The team secretaries, helped by the other players in their team, have to write down six words of five to six letters. Check to make sure that the words they choose are not too difficult.

A player from Team A then writes up the same number of dashes as there are letters in his or her team's first word. Team B has to guess what the letters are (and eventually what the word is) by calling out letters.

If Team B says a letter which **is** in the word, the player from Team A replaces the appropriate dash or dashes with the letter. If Team B says a letter which is **not** in the word, the player from Team A draws a part of a gallows, in the order in which the parts are numbered:

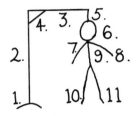

If the drawing of the gallows is completed (i.e. after eleven wrong guesses), Team A wins a point. If Team B guesses the word before the drawing is completed, Team B wins a point.

For example:

Team A's first word is *grass*. One player from Team A writes up: _ _ _ _ _
Team B says: E
Team A draws the base of the gallows because there is no E in grass: —
Team B says: A
Team A fills in: _ _ A _ _
Team B says: N

Team A draws:

Team B says: S
Team A fills in: _ _ A S S

And so on.

Hints: Practise pronouncing the alphabet before playing the game.
You could introduce the rule that the letter a team calls out stands even if they meant a different letter.
Play a practice round before playing properly.

SPELLING PUZZLE

Can you spell these words?

OTBLET

1. *BOTTLE*

RUTCAINS

2. ....

VIKSEN

3. ....

ZAEGMINAS

4. ....

HOSEWR

5. ....

YAJPAMS

6. ....

YIFFT

7. ....

UEQEU

8. ....

NEEXTIS

9. ....

SIBCUTIS

10. ....

SKEBNALT

11. ....

GINIDN MOOR

12. ....

CASUAPEN

13. ....

RORYL

14. ....

HACEB

15. ....

© Colin Granger and John Plumb 1993

27

Have got + a/some: He's got a pair of trainers.
They've got some glasses.

Photocopy pages 29 and 93 to play this game.

Divide the class into small teams of two to three players and appoint team secretaries. Hand out page 29 and give the teams two minutes to study and memorise the pictures. Then get the teams to cover or hand you back page 29. Hand out page 93 and go through the example with the class. Make sure the students understand the use of *he/she has got, they have got* and *a/some*. The team secretaries, helped by the rest of their team, then write down what the various people in the pictures have got. They must not look back at the first page while doing this. The team with the most correct sentences is the winner.

Alternatively, score 2 points if the sentences are both grammatically and factually correct, 1 point if only factually correct. The team with the most points is the winner.

ANSWERS:	1.	He's got a pair of trainers.
	2.	They've got some glasses.
	3.	She's got some books.
	4.	He's got a watch.
	5.	She's got a walkman.
	6.	He's got a tennis racket.
	7.	She's got a mobile phone.

LIST GAME

Have got + a/an/some: Carmen has got a diary. I've got some keys.

Begin the game by getting a student to hold up a possession and say what he or she has got, e.g. *I've got a diary.* Explain that the next player has to say what the first player has got and then hold up a possession of his or her own and make a new sentence, e.g. *Carmen has got a diary. I've got some keys.* The game continues with each player in turn trying to remember what the preceding players have got and then adding a new item of their own. Players get minus points if they *(a)* make a memory mistake, or *(b)* hesitate too long. Do not give minus points to players who make grammar mistakes - just correct the mistake and let the player continue. For example:

Player 1:	*I've got a diary.*
Player 2:	*Carmen has got a diary and I've got some keys.*
Player 3:	*Carmen has got a diary. Gerald has got some keys and I've got a pencil.*
Player 4:	*Carmen has got a diary. Gerald has got some keys. Sophia has got a pencil and I've got some pens.*
Player 5:	*Carmen has got a diary. Gerald has got some keys. Sophia has got a pen...* (Player 5 gets a minus point for making a memory mistake.)
Player 6:	(starting again) *I've got some stamps.*
Player 7:	*Trudi has got some stamps and I've got an envelope.*

And so on. The players with the least number of minus points at the end of the game are the winners.
Hints: Play a trial round before starting to award minus points.

MEMORY 3

1. Look at the picture for two minutes. Try to memorise their presents.

2. Turn the page over.

3. Answer the questions on the second page.

It's their birthday today. What presents have they got?

1.

2.

3.

4.

5.

6.

7.

NOW ANSWER THE QUESTIONS ON THE SECOND PAGE

Use these words:

pair of trainers   tennis racket

books   watch   walkman   mobile phone   glasses

OBSERVATION 2

Can (Requests): *Can you switch on the light?*

Divide the class into small teams of two to three players and appoint team secretaries. Set a ten-minute time limit for the team secretaries, helped by the rest of their team, to write the questions. The team with the most correct questions is the winner.

ANSWERS:		
	1.	Can you switch on the light?
	2.	Can you open the door?
	3.	Can you answer the telephone?
	4.	Can you pass me the telephone book?
	5.	Can you close the window?
	6.	Can you get me a coffee?
	7.	Can you switch off the computer?

REQUESTS

Can (Requests): *Can you clean the board?*

First, give a few examples yourself by requesting students to do things in the classroom situation, e.g. *ask a student to clean the board for you, fetch you something, open the window or door, switch on or off the light.* Then divide the class into teams of four to six players and appoint team secretaries. The team secretaries, helped by the rest of their team, should then write five different requests using different verbs. Go round as they do this checking that the questions are correct and possible to carry out in the classroom situation. Each team in turn then makes a request to a named player in the team next to them. They must choose a different player each time. The named player wins a point for his or her team if he or she understands and carries out the request. For example:

Player	(Team A):	*Angelica. Can you close the window?*
Angelica	(Team B):	*Sure.* (Angelica closes the window and wins a point for Team B).
Player	(Team B):	*Konrad. Can you fetch me the waste paper bin?*
Konrad	(Team C):	*I'm sorry. I don't understand.* (Team C doesn't get a point).
Player	(Team C):	*Manolo.Can you give this pen to Valerie?*
Manolo	(Team D):	*Of course.* (Manolo gives the pen to Valerie and wins a point for Team D).

The team with the most points is the winner.

O**B**SERVATION 2

Look at the picture of an office.
What are the people asking?

Use these verbs:

close   answer   get me   switch on   open   pass me   switch off

Write seven questions. Begin each sentence with 'Can you...'

1. Can you switch on the light?

2. ....

3. ....

4. ....

5. ....

6. ....

7. ....

© Colin Granger and John Plumb 1993

31

WHAT'S MISSING?

Have got + a/any: *It hasn't got a handle.*
They haven't got any headlights.

Divide the class into small teams of two to three players and appoint team secretaries. The team secretaries, helped by the other players in their team, have to write down as many sentences as they can in the two-minute time limit. The team with the most correct sentences is the winner.

ANSWERS:	1.	It hasn't got a dial.
	2.	They haven't got any headlights.
	3.	It hasn't got a handle.
	4.	It hasn't got a tail.
	5.	It hasn't got any taps.
	6.	It hasn't got a door.
	7.	They haven't got any saddles.
	8.	They haven't got any laces.

WHAT'S DIFFERENT?

Some/any : *There are some pencils.*
Countable/Uncountable Nouns: *There isn't any paper.*

You will need a large number of different objects for this game, e.g. *paper, pencils, pens, books, magazines, wool, sugar, cups* etc. Make sure that some of these things are **uncountable** nouns (e.g. *paper* and *wool*). Place some of the objects on a table or desk. Divide the class into two teams (Team A and Team B). Ask the players in Team A to look at what is on the table for one minute. Then, without Team A seeing, remove three objects (e.g. *paper, books, magazines*) and add three new objects (e.g. *pencils, sugar, cups*). Then ask Team A to come back and look at the table once more and say (*a*) what is missing; and (*b*) what is new:

> *There are some pencils.*
> *There isn't any paper.*
> *There aren't any books.*
> *There is some sugar.*

Score 2 points for each correct observation; but only 1 point if the grammar is wrong. Repeat with Team B. At the end, the team with the most points is the winner.

WHAT'S MISSING ?

There is a deliberate mistake in these pictures.
Find what is missing. You have two minutes.

1.

2.

3.

4.

5.

6.

7.

8.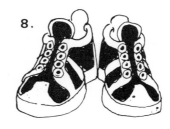

Use these words:
dial   headlights   laces   taps   handle   door   saddles   tail

1. *It hasn't got a dial.*

2. *They haven't got any headlights.*

3. ....

4. ....

5. ....

6. ....

7. ....

8. ....

ANIMAL QUIZ

Verb *to be*: *It's very big.*
Present Simple: *It lives in Africa.*
Have got: *It has got a long tail.*
Can (Ability): *It can run very fast.*

Divide the class into small teams of two to three players. The teams have to join the pictures of the animals to the descriptions. The first team to complete the quiz correctly is the winner.
Hints: You could get the players to write similar descriptions of other animals for the rest of the group to guess.

ANSWERS:	A8	B3	C4	D6	E7	F2	G5	H1

20 QUESTIONS – ANIMALS

Verb *to be*: *Is it a big animal? Yes, it is./No, It isn't.*
Present Simple: *Does it eat meat?*
Yes, it does./No, it doesn't.
Have got: *Has it got four legs? Yes, it has./No, it hasn't.*
Can (Ability): *Can it climb trees? Yes, it can./No, it can't.*

Write the name of an animal on a slip of paper. Explain that the class has to guess what animal you have written in 20 questions. Guide the class to ask questions with the following patterns:

Is it ...? Does it ...? Has it got ...? Can it ...?

Write up the patterns as they are introduced. Answer their questions with short form answers, i.e. *Yes, it is. No, it isn't*, etc.

Divide the class into two teams (Team A and Team B). Each team writes down the name of three animals. Check that there is no duplication of names. Team B then has 20 questions to find what Team A's first animal is. Each member of Team A takes it in turns to answer the questions.

Write up the score like this: If Team B gets the answer in fourteen questions, write: *Team B 14*. If Team B fails to guess what the animal is in twenty questions, write: *Team B 20*. Then it is Team A's turn to try to guess Team B's first animal, and so on with the other four animals. At the end, the team with the **lowest** score is the winner.

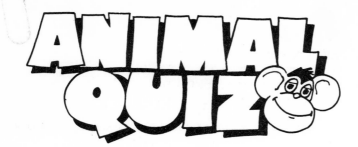

ANIMAL QUIZ

Join the picture to the description.

1. MONKEY

2. PENGUIN

3. MOUSE

4. SNAKE

5. ZEBRA

6. GIRAFFE

7. SEAGULL

8. ELEPHANT

A ☐ It's very big. It's strong. It is grey. It lives in Africa. It eats leaves. It has got four legs.

B ☐ It's very small. It has got a long tail. It lives in nearly all countries. It likes cheese.

C ☐ It is very long. It has not got any legs. It eats small animals. It is sometimes dangerous.

D ☐ It can run very fast. It has got a very long neck. It eats leaves. It has got four long legs.

E ☐ It can fly. It can dive. It's usually white. It eats fish and lives by the sea.

F ☐ It can swim in the sea and walk on the land. It cannot fly. It eats fish. It lives in very cold countries.

G ☐ It looks like a horse. It lives in Africa. It eats grass. It has got black and white stripes.

H ☐ It has got fingers. It can climb trees. It is brown. It lives on nuts and fruit. It lives in Africa and Asia.

MY AUNT FROM ...

Like + **Noun:** *She likes cheese,*
but she doesn't like meat.

Working individually or in pairs, the players have to write down what the aunt likes and dislikes. Write up their answers after asking how the nouns (*books, magazines,* etc.) are spelt:

She likes books, but she doesn't like magazines.
She likes coffee, but she doesn't like tea.

Introduce the phrase *double O, double E,* etc. In this way the players should be able to guess that the aunt only likes things if they are spelt with a **double letter.**

Hints: After they have found out the solution you could extend this game by asking the players to write down as many items that the aunt would like as they can think of, e.g.

What colours does she like? (The players write *green, yellow,* etc.)
What sports does she like? (*football, tennis,* etc.)
What languages does she like? (*Russian, Greek,* etc.)

And so on, with different categories.

ANSWERS:	1.	She likes *cheese*, but she doesn't like *meat*.
	2.	She likes *sheep*, but she doesn't like *cows*.
	3.	She likes *books*, but she doesn't like *magazines*.
	4.	She likes *chess*, but she doesn't like *cards*.
	5.	She likes *apples*, but she doesn't like *bananas*.
	6.	She likes *coffee*, but she doesn't like *tea*.
	7.	She likes *dresses*, but she doesn't like *skirts*.
	8.	She likes *spoons*, but she doesn't like *forks*.
	9.	She likes *doors*, but she doesn't like *windows*.
		She only likes things spelt with a double letter, e.g. ch**ee**se, sh**ee**p, b**oo**ks, etc.
		She comes from W**oo**llamalloo, you see!

MY AUNT FROM ... – extension

Like + **Infinitive:** *Does she like to cook?*
Yes, she likes to cook./
No, she doesn't like to cook.

Tell the class that you too have a rather peculiar aunt, this time from Edinburgh, who likes to do some things and dislikes doing others. By asking *Does she like …?* questions, the class has to find the logic behind her choice. The solution this time is that she only likes to do actions which begin with a **vowel**. For example:

Player:	*Does she like to eat?*
You:	*Yes, she likes to eat.*
Player:	*Does she like to read?*
You:	*No, she doesn't like to read.*
Player:	*Does she like to ask questions?*
You:	*Yes, she likes to ask questions.*

Tell anybody who you feel knows the answer to keep it to themselves for the moment and to carry on playing the game getting positive answers from you each time. You could also involve these players in helping you decide what the aunt likes and dislikes doing.

Play until most students have found the solution. You could then ask the players to try to invent an aunt of their own for the rest of the class to guess. For example:

My Aunt from Slough who only likes nouns spelt with **silent letters,** e.g. *blue, knives, dough.*
My Aunt from Hull who only likes verbs with **four letters,** e.g. *play, walk, open.*

Hints: Practise *Do you like* questions by playing one game with *Find out what I like* rather than *Find out what my aunt likes.*

MY AUNT FROM...

MY AUNT COMES FROM WOOLLAMALLOO IN AUSTRALIA. HERE ARE SOME OF THE THINGS SHE <u>LIKES</u> AND SOME OF THE THINGS SHE <u>DOESN'T LIKE</u>

She likes...

She doesn't like...

WRITE WHAT SHE LIKES AND WHAT SHE DOESN'T LIKE.

1. She likes cheese, but she doesn't like meat.

2. She likes sheep, but she doesn't like cows.

3. ....

4. ....

5. ....

6. ....

7. ....

8. ....

9. ....

NOW, LOOKING AT THE WORDS, CAN YOU GUESS WHY SHE LIKES SOME THINGS AND NOT OTHERS? REMEMBER THE <u>NAME</u> OF THE TOWN SHE COMES FROM.

Likes

books	magazines	apples
chess	cards	bananas
spoons	forks	
doors	windows	dressess skirts
coffee	tea	

SPOT THE DIFFERENCE 1

Present Continuous: *The woman is opening her umbrella.*

Working individually (or in pairs), the players write down the differences in what the people are doing between Picture A and Picture B. They should write **full** sentences to do this. Set a ten minute time limit. The player with the most correct sentences is the winner.

ANSWERS:	In picture B:	
	The woman is opening her umbrella.	The girl is eating an ice-cream.
	It is raining.	The man and the woman are coming out of the shop.
	The man is getting out of the car.	The man is looking at his watch.
	The man is smoking a pipe.	The woman is carrying one shopping bag.
	The man is reading a newspaper.	The woman is wearing a hat.
	The boy is running down the steps.	The man is getting on the bus.

NOISES OFF

Present Continuous: *Are you eating something?*
No, I'm not eating.

Some kind of screen is necessary for this game. You could construct one by putting two chairs on top of a table or desk and then covering them with a cloth or some coats. Each player, in turn, goes behind the screen to carry out an action which makes some recognisable sound, e.g. *brushing hair, writing, eating.* The rest of the class has to guess what is being done. For example:

Player:	*Are you eating something?*
Player behind screen:	*No, I'm not eating.*
Player:	*Are you drinking something?*
Player behind screen:	*No, I'm not drinking …*

Hints: You could vary this game by putting behind the screen a number of objects which the players could choose to use e.g. *a ball to bounce, a pin to drop, matches to strike, a knife and a pencil to sharpen, paper to fold, envelopes to open, a bottle to uncork.*

Spot the Difference 1

Compare the pictures. Write what is different in picture B.

Use these verbs:	read	eat	run down	wear	get on
rain	get out	smoke	come out of	look at	open	carry

The woman is opening her umbrella. It is raining.

....

....

....

....

39

WHOSE?

Possessive 's (Genitive): *They're Nick's chairs.*

Working individually (or in pairs), the players write down who the different objects belong to. The first player to do this correctly is the winner.

Hints: Practise *his/hers* by also asking:

> *Whose chairs are these?* *They're his.*
> *Whose uniform is this?* *It's hers.*
> etc.

ANSWERS:		
1.	They're Nick's chairs.	7. They're Teresa's rackets.
2.	It's Teresa's uniform.	8. They're Nick's books.
3.	It's Nick's house.	9. They're Teresa's brushes.
4.	It's Teresa's car.	10. They're Nick's magazines.
5.	They're Teresa's CDs.	11. It's Nick's camera.
6.	It's Teresa's flat.	

FAMILY TREE

Possessive Adjectives: *Harry is our grandson.*

Draw a family tree, e.g.

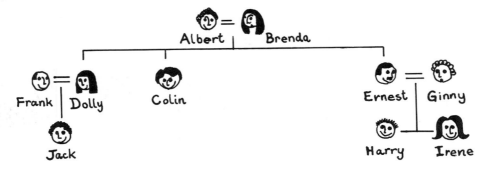

Then write up a list of family relationships:
grandparents, grandfather, grandmother, grandson, granddaughter; parents, father, mother, husband, wife; children, son, daughter, brother, sister; relatives, uncle, aunt, nephew, niece, cousin.
Make sure that everybody understands what the words mean. Divide the class into three or four teams. Explain that you are going to set them a number of relationship problems to solve. Give examples: Write up AB-H and E-D. Then, with the help of the class, work out and write up the following:

AB-H	Albert and Brenda say:	Harry is our grandson.
	Harry says:	Albert and Brenda are my grandparents.
	Albert and Brenda are his grandparents.	
	Harry is their grandson.	
E-D	Ernest says:	Dolly is my sister.
	Dolly says:	Ernest is my brother.
	Ernest is her brother.	
	Dolly is his sister.	

Set each team three problems. They have to write four sentences for each of their problems, for example:

Team 1:	HI-J,	A-E,	H-I
Team 2:	EG-I,	E-D,	E-G
Team 3:	CD-1	B-J,	D-C
Team 4:	D-HI,	B-C,	A-B

Give the teams fifteen to twenty minutes to carry out this task. A team secretary could write down the sentences for each team. The teams then read out their answers. Score 2 points for a correct sentence but only 1 point if the wrong possessive adjective is used. The team with the highest total is the winner.

WHOSE?

Read about Nick and Teresa.

Nick is 37. He is a photographer. Nick lives in a small, terraced house in South London. He works in Central London. He goes to work on the tube. He does not own a car. Nick does not like sport. He likes reading and watching television. His hobby is collecting antique furniture. He is also very interested in history.

Teresa is 28. She is a nurse. Teresa lives in a flat in Brighton. She works in a hospital outside Brighton. She drives to work every day. Teresa's hobby is painting. She is also interested in jazz and has got a big collection of records. She likes sport very much, especially tennis and squash.

Whose are these?

Use these words:					house
camera	compact discs		rackets		
flat	uniform	car	books	brushes	magazines	chairs

1. ...... They're Nick's chairs.

2. ...... It's Teresa's uniform.

3. ....

4. ....

5. ....

6. ....

7. ....

8. ....

9. ....

10. ....

11. ....

41

CONNECTIONS 1

Verb *to be* + Adjective: *He's thirsty.*
***Want to* + Infinitive:** *He wants to have a drink.*

Divide the class into small teams of two to three players. Appoint team secretaries. Set a ten minute time limit for the team secretaries, helped by the rest of their team, to write the sentences. The team with the most correct sentences is the winner.

ANSWERS:			
	1 D	He's thirsty.	He wants to have a drink.
	2 B	She's tired.	She wants to catch a bus.
	3 C	They're hot.	They want to go swimming.
	4 A	He's poor.	He wants to be rich.
	5 E	They're bored.	They want to play football.
	6 H	She's hungry.	She wants to order some food.
	7 G	He's cold.	He wants to turn on the heater.
	8 F	They're wet.	They want to stay inside.

INVENTION GAME

***Want to* + Infinitive:** *I want to play tennis.*

Choose a vocabulary area which your students are familiar with, e.g. *sports*. Begin the game by saying *I want to play tennis.* Explain that each player in turn has to say the same sentence but with a different sport. For example:

Player 1:	*I want to play football.*
Player 2:	*I want to play baseball.*
Player 3:	*I want to play golf.*

Players get minus points if they *(a)* are unable to think of a new item within the vocabulary area; *(b)* repeat a vocabulary item which has already been used; *(c)* use an inappropriate vocabulary item; or *(d)* hesitate too long. For example:

Player 1:	*I want to play football.*
Player 2:	*I want to play baseball.*
Player 3:	*I want to play golf.*
Player 4:	*I want to play skiing.* (Player 4 uses an inappropriate vocabulary item (*I want to go skiing*) and gets a minus point.)
Player 5:	*I want to play volleyball.*

And so on. Start a new round of the game with a different base sentence and a different vocabulary area as soon as players begin to run out of ideas, e.g. *I want to have a coke.* The player with the least number of minus points at the end of the game is the winner.

CONNECTIONS 1

What do these people want? Find the matching pictures. Then write two sentences.

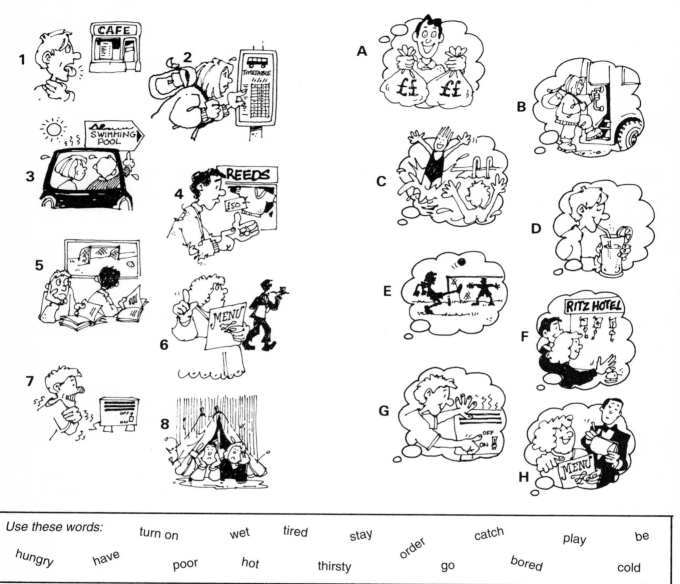

Use these words:

turn on   wet   tired   stay   order   catch   play   be

hungry   have   poor   hot   thirsty   go   bored   cold

1. *1 – D. He's thirsty. He wants to have a drink.*

2. ....

3. ....

4. ....

5. ....

6. ....

7. ....

8. ....

DESCRIPTIONS QUIZ

Have got: *He's got long dark hair.*
Present Continuous:*He's wearing a white shirt and a tie.*

Divide the class into small teams of two to three players. Appoint team secretaries. The team secretaries, helped by the other members of their team, find the correct description for each picture. The team which completes this task correctly in the shortest time is the winner.

ANSWERS:	1H	2B	3D	4E	5K	6G

EYE WITNESS

Have got: *She's got brown hair.*
Present Continuous: *She's wearing a blouse and a skirt.*

Take in a number of pictures of people taken from magazines. You will need three pictures for every three or four students in the class. Divide the class into teams of three to four players. Introduce the idea of being an eye witness to a crime. Give a set of three pictures of different people to each team, explaining that these people were seen at the scene of the crime and that the teams have to try to remember what the three people look like. Set a time limit of three minutes for them to do this. Then take back the pictures and interview each team in turn about the people in their pictures. For example:

> You: *What colour hair has the woman got? Is it long or short?*
> *Has she got brown eyes or blue eyes? What is she wearing?*
> *Is she wearing earrings? What colour is her blouse?*

You could award marks out of five for each of the pictures depending on how well the players answer.
Hints: You could get the students to take over your role as the interviewer.

DESCRIPTIONS QUIZ

Join the picture to the correct description.

A He's got long dark hair. He's wearing a white shirt and a tie.

B She's got short blonde hair. She's wearing a white blouse and jeans.

C He's got short fair hair and glasses. He's wearing a dark suit.

D He's got dark wavy hair and a moustache. He's wearing a sweater and jeans.

E She's got long dark hair. She's wearing a white dress.

F He's got dark straight hair. He's wearing a jacket and black sweater.

G She's got dark wavy hair. She's wearing a dark blouse and a white suit.

H He's got short dark hair. He's wearing a dark suit.

I She's got short dark hair. She's wearing a blouse and jeans.

J She's got long wavy hair. She's wearing a white T-shirt and white skirt.

K He's got long fair hair and a beard. He's wearing a white shirt and a tie.

L She's got long fair hair. She's wearing a jacket and a white skirt.

CATEGORIES 1

Was/Were: *It was cold. They were interesting.*

Working individually (or in pairs), the players write down sentences about the three pictures using the key words. Set a ten-minute time limit. The player with the most correct sentences is the winner.

ANSWERS:	What was the weather like?	It was cold/wet/windy/cloudy.
	What was the restaurant like?	It was crowded/expensive/uncomfortable/small.
	What were the people like?	They were interesting/charming/ intelligent/talkative.

20 QUESTIONS – FAMOUS PEOPLE

Was: *Was he European?*
Past Simple: *Did he live in this century?*

Discuss with the class what occupations well-known people can have. Write up a list: *scientist, writer, soldier, spy, actress, queen, artist*. Write the name of a famous **dead** personality on a slip of paper. Explain that the class has to guess *who* you have written in twenty questions. The questions have to be ones you can answer with *Yes* or *No*. Tell the class that it is better to ask general questions at first rather than random guesses: e.g. *Was he European?* is better than *Was he French? Did he live in this century?* is better than *Did he die ten years ago?*

Then divide the class into two teams (Team A and Team B). Tell each team to write down the names of three well-known, dead personalities. Check that the names they write are internationally famous. Also check that there is no duplication of names.
Team B then has twenty questions to find who Team A's first personality is. One player from Team A answers their questions. Write up the score like this: If Team B gets the answer in fourteen questions, write up: *Team B 14*. If Team B fails to get the answer in twenty questions, write up: *Team B 20*. Then it is Team A's turn to try to guess Team B's first name, and so on, with the other four names. At the end, the team with the **lowest** total is the winner.

WHAT'S DIFFERENT?

Was/Were + Prepositions of Place: *The pen was under the books.*
The pencils were on top of the file.

Place a large number of objects on a table or desk, e.g *two books, a pen, two pencils, a cassette, a file*, etc. Place the objects in different relationships to one another — *the pen under the book, the pencils on top of the file*, etc.

Give the first player one minute to study how the different objects are arranged on the table. Then, without the player seeing, alter the position of five objects. The player then comes back and has to say what is different: *The pen was under the books. The pencils were on top of the file.* Score 1 point for each correct observation. The second player then studies the new arrangement for one minute, and so on. Change the position of five objects for each player. At the end, the player with the most points is the winner.

46

CATEGORIES 1

Describe last weekend.

Write four sentences for each picture.

You went for a walk in the country.

WHAT WAS THE WEATHER LIKE?

It was cold.
....
....
....

You went to a restaurant for dinner.

WHAT WAS THE RESTAURANT LIKE?

....
....
....
....

You went to a party where you met a lot of people.

WHAT WERE THE PEOPLE LIKE?

They were interesting.
....
....
....

Use these words:

expensive   uncomfortable   windy   intelligent

small   crowded

wet   cloudy   interesting   charming   cold   talkative

COMPARATIVE QUIZ

Comparative: *The Pacific Ocean is bigger than the Atlantic Ocean.*

Divide the class into two teams (Team A and Team B). Ask Team A to think of a sentence about Picture 1, e.g. *The Parthenon is older than the Colosseum.* Then ask Team B to think of a sentence for Picture 2, and so on with the other seven pictures. Score 2 points for each correct answer; 1 point if the grammar is incorrect. At the end, the team with the most points is the winner.

ANSWERS:	1.	The Pacific Ocean is bigger than the Atlantic Ocean. (The Pacific Ocean is 165m km in area.)
	2.	The Parthenon is older than the Colosseum. (The Parthenon was begun in 447 B.C.; the Colosseum was built between A.D. 72–82.)
	3.	Venus is nearer the sun than Mars. (Venus is 108m km from the sun; Mars is 228m km.)
	4.	Russia is larger than China. (Russia has approximately 10% of the world's land surface; China approximately 7%.)
	5.	The Suez Canal is longer than the Panama Canal. (The Suez Canal is 162 km long; the Panama Canal is 82 km long.)
	6.	Mount Everest is higher than Mount Fuji. (Mount Fuji is 3776 m high; Mount Everest is 8848 m high.)
	7.	A snail is slower than a tortoise. (A snail travels at 0.05 km/h; a tortoise at 0.127 km/h.)
	8.	The Sahara desert is hotter than the Gobi desert.
	9.	A giraffe is taller than an elephant.

COMPARATIVE QUIZ – extension

Comparative: *A mile is longer than a kilometre.*

Continue, as above, by getting each team to write a number of similar problems for the other team to solve, e.g. *kilometre, mile — long; Tokyo, New York — big population; Mr X, Mr Y (two politicians) — old; car A, car B — fast; product X, product Y — expensive; place A, place B — far; book X, book Y — more pages; drink A, drink B — strong.*

Check that the problems they write are not too difficult and that the team that has written the problem knows the answer. Also make sure that there is no duplication of questions. Alternatively, prepare a number of problems yourself to put to the two teams.

COMPARATIVE QUIZ

Compare the following.

1. PACIFIC OCEAN / ATLANTIC OCEAN — BIG

2. Parthenon / Colosseum — OLD

3. Mars / Venus — NEARER THE SUN

4. Russia / China — LARGE

5. Suez Canal / Panama Canal — LONG

6. Mount Fuji / Mount Everest — HIGH

7. Tortoise / Snail — SLOW

8. Sahara Desert / Gobi Desert — HOT

9. — TALL

1. The Pacific Ocean is bigger than the Atlantic Ocean.

2. ....

3. ....

4. ....

5. ....

6. ....

7. ....

8. ....

9. ....

SUPERLATIVE QUIZ

Superlative: *The Pacific is the largest ocean.*

Divide the class into two teams (Team A and Team B). Team A asks Team B the first question. Team B can consult together before answering. Then Team B asks Team A the second question, and so on with the other four questions. Score 2 points for each correct answer; 1 point if the grammar is incorrect. At the end, the team with the most points is the winner.

ANSWERS:			
	1.	Pacific	(165 million km in area)
	2.	Nile	(6670 km long)
	3.	Cheetah	(101 km/h)
	4.	Sears Tower	(548 m high)
	5.	Vatican City	(44 hectares)
	6.	Chinese	(575 million speakers; English has 360 million speakers.)
	7.	Chang	(at least 75,000,000 people have this name)
	8.	University of Fez (Morocco)	(founded AD859)

SUPERLATIVE QUIZ – extension

Superlative: *Which city has the biggest population in the world?*

Continue, as above, by getting each team to write a number of questions for the other team to answer, e.g. *Which city has the biggest population in the world? What is the largest island? What is the highest mountain? What is the biggest country?* etc. Check that the questions they write are not too difficult, and that the team that has written the question knows the answer. Also make sure that there is no duplication of questions. Alternatively, prepare a number of questions yourself to put to the two teams.

SUPERLATIVE QUIZ

Put a ☑ next to the correct answer.

1. Which is the largest ocean?

Pacific ☐

Atlantic ☐

Indian ☐

2. Which is the longest river?

Mississippi ☐

Nile ☐

Amazon ☐

3. Which is the fastest animal?

antelope ☐

horse ☐

cheetah ☐

4. Which is the tallest building?

Eiffel Tower ☐

Sears Tower (Chicago) ☐

Empire State Building (New York) ☐

5. Which is the smallest country?

Vatican City ☐

Monaco ☐

Andorra ☐

6. Which is the most spoken language?

Spanish ☐

English ☐

Chinese ☐

7. Which is the most common family name?

Chang ☐

Smith ☐

Kim ☐

8. Which is the oldest university?

Fez (Morocco) ☐

Oxford (Britain) ☐

Sorbonne (France) ☐

Question Words + Present Tense Questions:
How old are you? Where do you come from?

Divide the class into small teams of two to three players and appoint team secretaries. Set a time limit of three minutes for the team secretaries, helped by the other members of their team, to match the questions to the answers. The team with the most correct answers is the winner.

Hints: Practise the questions and answers by afterwards getting the players to read out the questions for other players to answer.

ANSWERS:	A6	B7	C8	D4	E1	F2	G3	H5

20 QUESTIONS – ANIMAL, VEGETABLE AND MINERAL

Present Tense Questions: *Is it natural?*
Do we use it every day?
Can we eat it?

Explain the categories *animal, vegetable* and *mineral* and give examples:

Animal:	all forms of animal life or anything of animal origin.
Vegetable:	all forms of vegetable life or anything of vegetable origin.
Mineral:	all forms of inorganic life or anything of inorganic origin.

This jacket is animal.	*It's made of wool from a sheep.*
This chair is vegetable.	*t's made of wood from a tree.*
This ring is mineral.	*It's made of gold.*

Check that the class understands the three categories by asking them to categorise different objects, e.g. *gold* (m), *a bottle* (m), *a grape* (v), *a bank note* (v), *a dog* (a), *a hair* (a).

Write the name of an object on a slip of paper. Say what category the object belongs to. Explain that the class has to guess what object you have written in twenty questions. The questions have to be ones you can answer with *Yes* or *No*. Tell the class that it is better to ask general questions at first (e.g. *Is it natural? Do we use it everyday? Can we eat it?*) rather than random guesses. Divide the class into two teams (Team A and Team B). Tell each team to write down three objects, one for each category. Check that the objects they choose are not a combination of categories (e.g. *a can of beer*).

Encourage humorous objects such as *false teeth, Mr X's ears* (a student in the class), *the flea that bit me last night, Miss Z's lipstick,* etc.Team A then begins by saying the category of their first object. Team B has twenty questions to find what the object is. A player from Team A (probably assisted by you) answers the questions. Write up the score like this: If Team B gets the answer in fourteen questions, write up: *Team B 14.* If Team B fails to guess the object in twenty questions, write up: *Team B 20.* Then it is Team A's turn to try to guess Team B's first object, and so on, with the other four objects. At the end, the team with the **lowest** total is the winner.

CONNECTIONS 2

Connect the question with the answer.

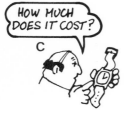

A—6

....
....
....
....

....
....
....
....

53

SPOT THE DIFFERENCE 2

Prepositions of Movement: *up, down, out of, into, off, onto*

Present Continuous: *The man is going up the escalator.*

Working individually or in pairs, the players write down the differences in what the people are doing between picture A and picture B. They should write complete sentences to do this. Set a ten-minute time limit. The player with the most correct sentences at the end is the winner.

ANSWERS:
In picture B...
The man is going up the escalator.
The two women are coming out of the restaurant.
The woman is putting books onto a shelf.
Two men are going into the lift.
The boy and a girl are coming down the escalator.
The girl is getting out of a toy car.
The boy is getting into a toy car.
The man is going into the restaurant.
The woman is putting a train into a box.
The customer is taking money out of her purse.

FOLLOW MY NEIGHBOUR

Prepositions of Movement: *towards, across, to, out, out of, onto, into*

Imperative: *Walk towards me. Don't take the book off the desk.*

Get individual or pairs of students to carry out a series of instructions in the classroom situation. For example:

You: *Stand up. Walk towards me. Now walk across the room to the door.*
Open the door. Don't go out of the room. Turn round. Pick up the red book.
Put it onto the next desk. Pick up the pen. Put it in your pocket.

You could give ten instructions to each individual player or pair of players and award minus points for each instruction they fail to carry out correctly. The player with the least number of minus points at the end of the game is the winner.

Hints: You could get the students to take over your role as the instructor.

Spot the Difference 2

Compare the pictures. Write what is different in picture B.

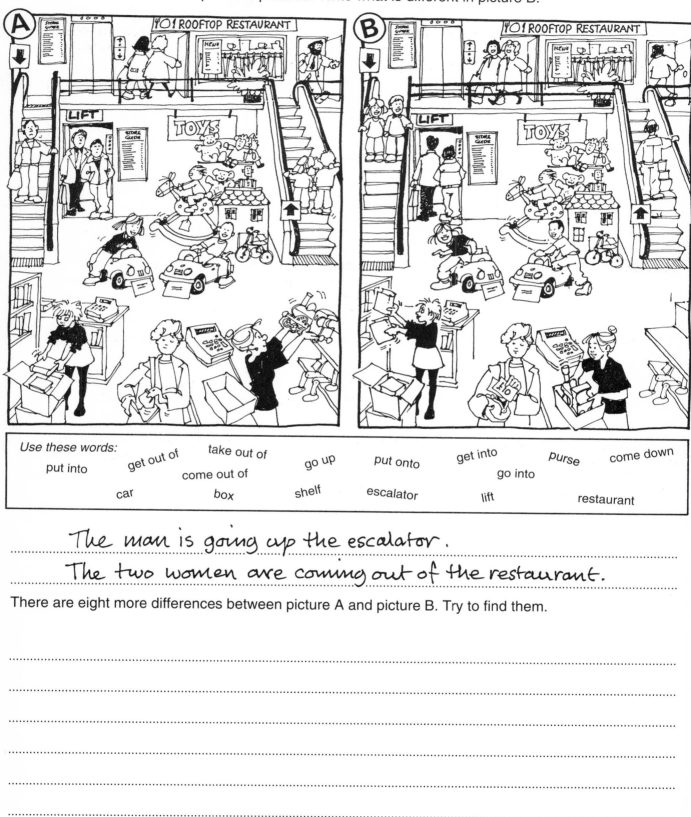

Use these words:

put into · get out of · take out of · go up · put onto · get into · purse · come down · come out of · go into · car · box · shelf · escalator · lift · restaurant

The man is going up the escalator.

The two women are coming out of the restaurant.

There are eight more differences between picture A and picture B. Try to find them.

....

....

....

....

....

....

....

....

OBSERVATION 3

Have (got) to (Obligation): *She's got to get some money*

Divide the class into small teams of two to three players and appoint team secretaries. Set a ten-minute time limit for the team secretaries, helped by the rest of their team, to write the sentences. The team with the most correct sentences is the winner.

ANSWERS:
1. She's got to get some money.
2. She's got to buy some food.
3. She's got to post some letters.
4. She's got to go to the dentist's.
5. She's got to collect some dry-cleaning.
6. She's got to pay some bills.
7. She's got to take back a video.
8. She's got to mend some sunglasses.

BRAINSTORMING

Have (got) to (Obligation): *You have (got) to train every day.*

Divide the class into small teams of two to three players and appoint team secretaries. Write up the name of a job on the board, e.g. *an athlete,* and explain that the team secretaries, helped by the rest of their team, write down as many *You have (got) to ...* sentences expressing things people have to do or be if they want to be successful in that particular kind of work. For example, the teams would perhaps write down:

You have (got) to train every day.
You have (got) to be competitive.
You have (got) to eat the right kind of food.
You have (got) to get plenty of sleep.

Set a five-minute time limit. The teams then read out their ideas in turn. Get the team secretaries to cross out any ideas on their list which are the same or similiar (e.g. *You have (got) to train every day. You have (got) to be fit*). Disallow ideas which haven't got a strong enough connection with the job. At the end, the team with the most ideas left is the winner.

You could then play further rounds with different jobs, for example: *a politician, a teacher, a children's nanny, a racing driver, a diplomat, an actor/actress.*

OBSERVATION 3

It is Saturday the 11th of May.
Nicola has a lot of things to do today.

Look at the picture. What has she got to do?

Use these words:							
buy	post	go	get	mend	collect	pay	take back
bills	letters	food	dentist's	dry-cleaning	money	sunglasses	video

1. She's got to get some money.

2. ....

3. ....

4. ....

5. ....

6. ....

7. ....

8. ....

DETECTIVE 'ALIBI'

Past Simple: *On Friday I travelled by tube to Heathrow Airport.*

Working individually (or in pairs), the players have to complete Anderson's statement giving details of his alibi. Set a ten-minute time limit. The first player to do this correctly is the winner.

ANSWERS:	On Friday I *travelled* by tube to *Heathrow Airport*. I *bought* some *magazines* at the airport. I then *flew* to *Edinburgh* on a British Airways flight. I *had* dinner at the *Taj Mahal* restaurant in Edinburgh. After dinner I *saw* a film at the Odeon Cinema. My ticket *cost* £5.00. I *stayed* at the Cumberland Hotel in Room *351*. On Saturday morning I *hired* a car and *drove* to St Andrews. I *paid* a deposit of *£40.00*. In the afternoon I *went* fishing. In the evening I *returned* to Edinburgh. On Sunday morning I *caught* the 10.55 *train* to London. I *arrived* back in London at 17.05.

THE LONG SENTENCE GAME

Past Simple: *I went to town and saw a film.*

Begin the game by saying *I went to town and saw a film*. Explain that the first player has to repeat your sentence and add something new, e.g. *I went to town, saw a film and bought a newspaper*. The game continues with each player in turn trying to remember what the last player said, and then adding something new to the story. Players get minus points if they (*a*) make a memory mistake; or (*b*) hesitate too long. Do not give minus points for grammar mistakes — just correct the mistake and allow the player to continue.

Example round with a group of five players:

Player 1:	*I went to town and saw a film.*
Player 2:	*I went to town, saw a film and bought a newspaper.*
Player 3:	*I went to town, saw a film, bought a newspaper and had lunch.*
Player 4:	*I went to town, bought a newspaper* … (This player gets a minus point because of a memory mistake.)
Player 5:	*I went to town, saw a film, bought a newspaper, had lunch and parked my car.*
Player 1:	*I went to town* … etc.

And so on. When the story becomes too difficult to remember, you could then begin a new round of the game with a different situation, e.g. *I went to the seaside and swam in the sea …* . The player with the least number of minus points at the end of the game is the winner.

Hints: Play a trial round before playing properly.

DETECTIVE 'ALIBI'

The police believe that this man took part in a robbery in London last weekend. He tells them that he was not in London at the weekend. His alibi is that he was in Scotland.

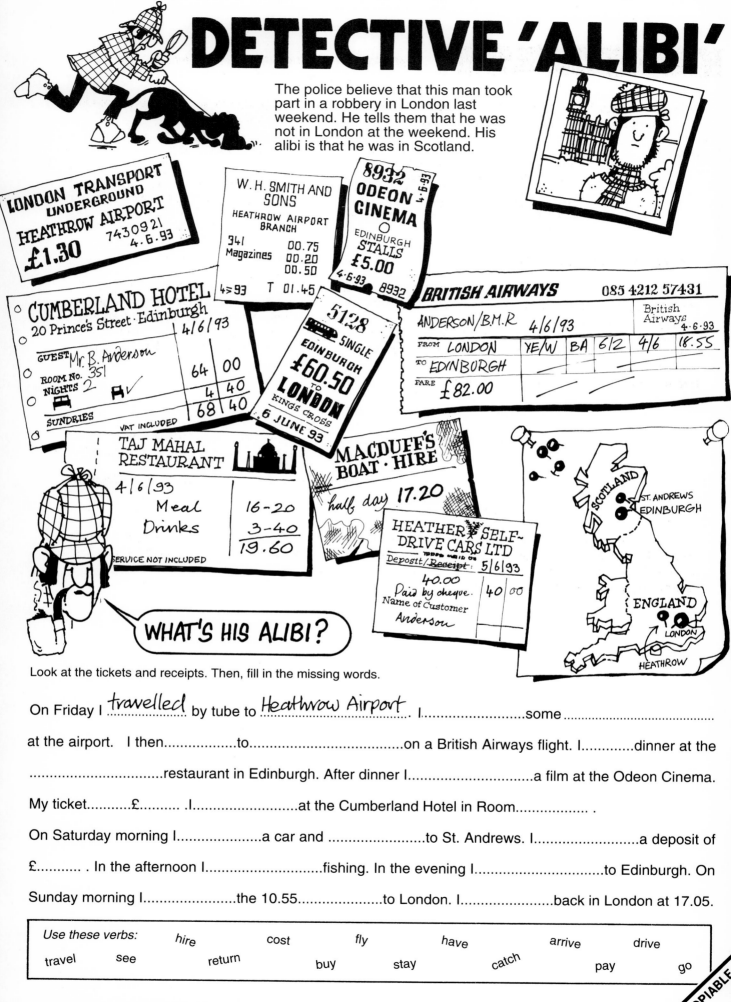

LONDON TRANSPORT UNDERGROUND
HEATHROW AIRPORT
£1.30   7430921
4.6.93

W. H. SMITH AND SONS
HEATHROW AIRPORT BRANCH
341   00.75
Magazines   00.20
              00.50
4>93   T 01.45

8932 ODEON CINEMA
EDINBURGH
STALLS
£5.00
4.6.93   8932

CUMBERLAND HOTEL
20 Prince's Street · Edinburgh
4/6/93
GUEST Mr. B. Anderson
ROOM No. 351
NIGHTS 2   64 00
               4 40
SUNDRIES   68 40
VAT INCLUDED

5128 SINGLE EDINBURGH £60.50 TO LONDON KINGS CROSS 6 JUNE 93

BRITISH AIRWAYS   085 4212 57431
ANDERSON/B.M.R   4/6/93   British Airways 4.6.93
FROM LONDON   YE/W BA 6/2 4/6 18.55
TO EDINBURGH
FARE £82.00

TAJ MAHAL RESTAURANT
4/6/93
Meal   16-20
Drinks   3-40
              19.60
SERVICE NOT INCLUDED

MACDUFF'S BOAT · HIRE
half day 17.20

HEATHER SELF-DRIVE CARS LTD
Deposit/Receipt: 5/6/93
40.00
Paid by cheque.   40 00
Name of Customer
Anderson

(map: SCOTLAND, ST. ANDREWS, EDINBURGH, ENGLAND, LONDON, HEATHROW)

WHAT'S HIS ALIBI?

Look at the tickets and receipts. Then, fill in the missing words.

On Friday I _travelled_ by tube to _Heathrow Airport_. I........................some ....
at the airport.   I then.................to.....................................on a British Airways flight. I.............dinner at the
...............................restaurant in Edinburgh. After dinner I.............................a film at the Odeon Cinema.
My ticket...........£.......... .I........................at the Cumberland Hotel in Room................. .
On Saturday morning I.....................a car and ....to St. Andrews. I..........................a deposit of
£.......... . In the afternoon I...........................fishing. In the evening I...............................to Edinburgh. On
Sunday morning I.....................the 10.55.....................to London. I.......................back in London at 17.05.

Use these verbs:	hire	cost	fly	have	arrive	drive
travel	see	return	buy	stay	catch	pay	go

59

DO-IT-YOURSELF QUIZ

Need + **Noun:** *She needs a hammer.*

Working individually (or in pairs), the players write down what the people in the pictures need to carry out the job they are doing. Set a time limit of six minutes. The player who writes the most correct sentences is the winner.

ANSWERS:		
	1. She needs a hammer.	7. She needs a nail.
	2. He needs some glue.	8. They need some bricks.
	3. They need some paint.	9. She needs a spade.
	4. He needs a saw.	10. They need some wallpaper.
	5. They need a ladder.	11. He needs a brush.
	6. He needs a screwdriver.	12. He needs a lawnmower.

ACTION GAME

Want + **Infinitive:** *I want to post a letter.*
Need + **Noun:** *You need a stamp.*

Begin by saying *I want to post a letter.* Explain that the next player has to think of something you need to do this action (e.g. *You need a stamp.*) and then say a new *I want to …* sentence for the next student. For example:

Player 1:	*I want to post a letter.*
Player 2:	*You need a stamp. I want to drive my car.*
Player 3:	*You need some petrol. I want to sharpen my pencil.*

The game continues in this way, like a chain drill round the class. Players get minus points if they *(a)* can't think of an appropriate *You need …* sentence; or *(b)* hesitate too long.
Example round with a group of five players:

Player 1:	*I want to post a letter.*
Player 2:	*You need a stamp. I want to drive my car.*
Player 3:	*You need some petrol. I want to sharpen a pencil.*
Player 4:	(This player can't think of a response and so gets a minus point.)
Player 5:	*You need a knife. I want to open the door.*
Player 1:	*You need a key. I want to …*

And so on. The player with the least number of minus points at the end of the game is the winner.
Hints: Play a trial round before playing properly.

DO-IT-YOURSELF QUIZ

What do these people need to do the job?

Use these words: glue   bricks   wallpaper   paint
hammer   ladder   nail   spade   screwdriver   saw   brush   lawnmower

1. She needs a hammer.

2. He needs some glue.

3. ....

4. ....

5. ....

6. ....

7. ....

8. ....

9. ....

10. ....

11. ....

12. ....

61

PICNIC

Going to **Future:** *I'm going to take a radio.*
Can **(Permission):** *You can come. You can't come.*

Ask the class what each student in the picture is going to take on the picnic, e.g. *Brian's going to take a banana.* At the same time, ask the class who, according to the students' teacher, is allowed to go on the picnic. For example:

> *Brian's going to take a banana. He can come.*
> *Connie's going to take a radio. She can't come.*

Then ask the class if anybody can see the logic behind Angela's choice of participants (i.e. She has decided that only students who say an object beginning with the **same letter as the initial letter of their name** can come on the picnic.) If nobody in the class can guess, ask them to join in the game by saying what **they** are going to take on the picnic, e.g.

> Gisella: *I'm going to take a book.*
> You: *You can't come.*
> Henry: *I'm going to take a hamburger.*
> You: *You can come.*

And so on, round the class.
Tell anybody who you feel knows the answer to keep it to themselves for the moment, and to carry on playing the game getting positive answers from you each time. You could also involve these players in helping you decide who can come on the picnic. Play until most students have found the solution.

ANSWERS:	Brian, Simon, May and Lucy are all bringing something beginning with the first letter of their name. (Brian — a **b**anana, Simon — a **s**poon, May — a **m**agazine, Lucy — a **l**emon.)

PICNIC – extension

Going to **Future:** *I'm going to play tennis.*
Can **(Permission):** *You can come. You can't come.*

Play the game with different rules, e.g. players can only come on the picnic if they are going to do an action which begins with a vowel:

> Player 1: *I'm going to play tennis.*
> You: *You can't come.*
> Player 2: *I'm going to eat a sandwich.*
> You: *You can come.*
> Player 3: *I'm going to drink a coke.*
> You: *You can't come.*

Some other rules:
Players can come only if they take an object with one syllable.
Players can come only if they do an action which is spelt with four letters.

Angela is a teacher. She is going on a picnic and wants to take some of her students. She cannot take everyone as her car is too small. To decide who can come she asks...

63

MEMORY 4

Past Simple: *No he didn't. Yes he did.*

Photocopy pages 65 and 94 to play this game.

Divide the class into small teams of two to three players and appoint team secretaries. Hand out page 65 and give the teams two minutes to study and memorise the pictures. Then get the teams to cover or hand you back page 65. Hand out page 94 and go through the example with the class. The team secretaries, helped by the rest of their team, write down the answers to the questions on page 94. They must not look at the first page while doing this. The team with the most correct answers is the winner.

Hints: Practise *he didn't* sentences by getting the class to say what Frank didn't do this morning, e.g.:

He didn't switch off the light.
He didn't close the window.
etc.

ANSWERS:					
1.	No, he didn't.	7.	Yes, he did.	13.	No, he didn't.
2.	Yes, he did.	8.	No, he didn't.	14.	No, he didn't.
3.	No, he didn't.	9.	No, he didn't.		
4.	Yes, he did.	10.	Yes, he did.		
5.	No, he didn't.	11.	Yes, he did.		
6.	Yes, he did.	12.	Yes, he did.		

CAN'T REMEMBER STORY

Past Simple: *Did he get up at seven?*
He got up at a quarter to twelve.

Explain to the class that it was Frank's birthday yesterday (that is why he was in such a rush this morning), and that you are going to tell them what Frank did on this very special day. Begin to tell the story, then break off as though you can't remember:

You:	*Yesterday was Frank's birthday. In the morning he got up at ... er ... he got up at ... I'm sorry, I can't remember. Ask me 'Did he get up at ...?'*
Player:	*Did he get up at seven?*
You:	*No, he didn't get up at seven.*
Player:	*Did he get up at ten?*
You:	*No, he didn't get up at ten.*
Player:	*Did he get up at a quarter to twelve?*
You:	*Yes, he did. He got up at a quarter to twelve.*

Guide the players to the right answer by saying a definite *No* if they are way off the mark, and an encouraging *No* if they are getting warm. (If nobody can guess, accept any reasonable alternative as the 'correct' answer.)

Yesterday was Frank's birthday. In the morning he got up at a quarter to twelve. For his breakfast he had ... er, he had ... I'm sorry, I can't remember. Ask me 'Did he have ...?'

When they have found out what Frank had, begin again, retelling the story in full each time with the help of the class, and breaking off at the appropriate points for them to guess what happened.

The complete story

Yesterday was Frank's birthday. In the morning he got up at ... a quarter to twelve. For breakfast he had ... fish and chips. In the afternoon he went to ... the zoo. He rode on ... a camel and bought ... an ice-cream. In the evening he went to the cinema and saw ... a horror film.

MEMORY 4

Frank is waiting at the bus stop. It's 8.20 in the morning. Frank is going to work.
Look at the picture of Frank's flat. He was having breakfast there a few moments ago.

 1. Look at this picture for two minutes.

 2. Turn the page over.

 3. Answer the questions on the second page.

ANSWER THE QUESTIONS ON THE SECOND PAGE.

© Colin Granger and John Plumb 1993

65

PHOTOCOPIABLE

Past Simple: *People didn't wear jeans.*

Divide the class into small teams of two to three players and appoint team secretaries. Give the teams eight minutes to spot the deliberate mistakes and for the team secretaries, with the help of the rest of their team, to write down the answers in complete sentences. The team with the most correct sentences is the winner.

Hints: Afterwards you could ask the class what people **did** wear, **did** write with, etc. in 1850.

ANSWERS:	People didn't watch television/TV.	People didn't eat hamburgers.
	People didn't listen to disco music.	People didn't have computers.
	People didn't use vacuum cleaners.	People didn't drink Coke.

YOU DO IT LIKE THIS

Past Simple: *You didn't turn off the tap.*

Give each player quite a complex task to mime, e.g. *cleaning his or her teeth, starting a car, doing the washing up, making an omelette, shaving, changing a wheel, telephoning from a coin box.*
Each player in turn then mimes his or her task. Explain that it is not important if their mime is not very good but that they should try to represent **all** the different actions associated with their task. (e.g. *cleaning teeth — turning on tap, unscrewing top from toothpaste, picking up toothbrush, putting it under the tap,* etc.)
The rest of the class watch each mime and say afterwards what, in their opinion, wasn't represented, e.g.

You didn't spit out the water.
You didn't turn off the tap.

The player who mimes a task where nobody can make such comments is the winner.

DETECTIVE STORY–
'ROMEO AND JULIET'

Past Simple: *Did somebody break a glass?*
Were they murdered?

Read the story to the class, explaining any difficult vocabulary. Explain that the class must play detectives and find the solution to the problem.

The story

> *Romeo and Juliet are lying dead on the floor of the bedroom. There is some broken glass and some water on the floor. The door of the room is locked. The window is open.*

The class then ask you questions to find the solution to the story. They can only ask questions which have *Yes/No* answers, e.g. *Were they murdered? Did somebody break a glass?* Give hints to elicit questions, e.g.

> *Ask me questions about the broken glass. Was the glass from a flower vase?* etc.
> *Ask me questions about the water on the floor.*
> *Ask me questions about the open window.*
> *Ask me questions about how they died.*

The solution

> *Romeo and Juliet are goldfish. A cat came through the open window and tried to fish them out of the bowl with its paw. The bowl fell off the table and smashed on the floor. The cat leapt out of the window because of the noise, leaving Romeo and Juliet to die on the floor from suffocation.*

OBSERVATION 4

There are some deliberate mistakes in this nineteenth century family scene.

There are seven mistakes. Can you find them?

Use these verbs:						
wear	watch	use	drink	eat	listen to	have

1. .... *People didn't wear jeans.* ....

2. ....

3. ....

4. ....

5. ....

6. ....

7. ....

CATEGORIES 2

Both/All: They're both capital cities.
They're all directions.

Working individually (or in pairs), the players write sentences placing the 28 words into ten categories. The first player to do this correctly is the winner.

ANSWERS:
1. London, Washington. They're both capital cities.
2. North, South, East, West. They're all directions.
3. Carpenter, secretary, mechanic. They're all jobs.
4. Bathroom, kitchen. They're both rooms.
5. Fourth, second, third, sixth. They're all numbers.
6. Onions, potatoes. They're both vegetables.
7. Football, golf, tennis. They're all sports.
8. Cat, lion, monkey. They're all animals.
9. Greengrocer's, chemist's, supermarket. They're all shops.
10. Lorry, bus. They're both vehicles.

SIMILARITIES GAME

Both/All: They both speak English.
They're all ways of cooking food.

Ask each player in turn to state some sort of similarity between two or more words, e.g.

You:	*What can you tell me about an Australian and an American?*
Player 1:	*They both speak English.*
You:	*What can you tell me about boiling, frying and baking?*
Player 2:	*They're all ways of cooking food.*

Score 2 points for each answer; 1 point if *both* or *all* are wrongly used. At the end, the player with the most points is the winner.

Sample questions (adapt to the knowledge of your class).

Capital cities:	Paris, London, Washington
Materials:	wool, cotton
Cars:	a Mini, a Toyota, a Golf, a Jaguar
Vegetable:	peas, beans
Ports:	Hamburg, Liverpool, New York
Rooms:	kitchen, bathroom
Fuels:	coal, oil
Meat:	beef, pork, lamb, chicken
Fruit:	orange, lemon, apple
Actors:	Gerard Depardieu, Robert de Niro, Arnold Schwarzennegger
Trees:	oak, beech
Scientists:	Einstein, Galileo, Copernicus

CATEGORIES 2

Find the words for each category.
Write a sentence using **both** or **all**.

1.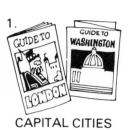
CAPITAL CITIES

2.
DIRECTIONS

3. JOBS

4.
ROOMS

5.
NUMBERS

6.
VEGETABLES

7.
SPORTS

8.
ANIMALS

9.
SHOPS

10.
VEHICLES

Use these words: monkey   carpenter   third   North   lorry   bus   golf
football   cat   East   fourth   London   tennis   secretary   South
bathroom   supermarket   chemist's   greengrocer's   West   Washington   mechanic
sixth   second   potatoes   lion   kitchen   onions

---

1. *London, Washington. They're both capital cities.*

2. *North, South, East, West. They're all directions.*

3. ....

4. ....

5. ....

6. ....

7. ....

8. ....

9. ....

10. ....

OBSERVATION 5

***Going to* Future:** *She's going to play tennis.*

Divide the class into small teams of two to three players and appoint team secretaries. Give the teams ten minutes to study the picture and for the team secretaries, helped by the rest of the players in their team, to write down sentences about what Nicola is going to do at the weekend. The team with the most correct sentences is the winner.

Hints: You could also get the teams to point out the evidence for their statements, e.g. *She's going to play tennis because she's taking her tennis things.*

ANSWERS:	1.	She's going to take some photographs.
	2.	She's going to wash her hair.
	3.	She's going to learn Spanish.
	4.	She's going to write some letters.
	5.	She's going to play tennis.
	6.	She's going to travel by train.
	7.	She's going to go to a concert..
	8.	She's going to go swimming
	9.	She's going to read a detective story.

JUST ABOUT

***Going to* Future:** *Are you going to wash your hands?*

Tell the class that they have to guess what you are **just about** to do — then mime the preparatory actions for *having a bath* (e.g. *putting in the plug, turning on the taps*). At the same time the class asks you questions to try to find out what you are going to do, e.g. *Are you going to wash your hands? Are you going to clean your teeth?* Shake your head if their guesses are wrong and continue the mime — *testing the temperature of the water, taking off your dressing gown, stepping into the bath* — until somebody guesses what you are going to do. Your mime does not have to be good to do this activity — the more amateur the mime the more questions will have to be asked. But it is important that the action itself is **not** mimed but only the preparatory actions leading up to it. Then write an action on a slip of paper and hand it to the player who guessed your mime. He or she then mimes that action for the rest of the class to guess.

Some example actions:

> *You are just about to drive away in your car.*
> *You are just about to go to sleep.*
> *You are just about to kiss somebody.*
> *You are just about to light a fire.*

Continue in this way, with either you or the player whose mime has just been guessed, writing a new action for the next player to mime.

DRAWING GAME

***Going to* Future:** *You're going to draw a house.*

Begin to draw a simple line drawing (for example: a car).

Stop after each stage to allow the class to try and guess what you are going to draw: *You're going to draw a house, You're going to draw a table,* etc.
Shake your head in reply until somebody guesses the right answer or you finish the drawing.
Continue with other simple line drawings, e.g.

OBSERVATION 5

Nicola is going away for the weekend. Find out what she is going to do by looking at the picture.

1.
2.
3. SPEAK IT SPANISH COURSE
4.
5.
6. LONDON TO MANCHESTER
7. FREEMASONS · HALL · DO · CONCERT B22 £4.00
8.
9. DETECTIVE STORY NOT A CLUE

Use these verbs:							
play	go	go swimming	wash	write	travel	learn	take	read

1. She's going to take some photographs.
2. She's going to wash her hair.
3. ....
4. ....
5. ....
6. ....
7. ....
8. ....
9. ....

71

USA QUIZ

Question Words + Present and Past Tense

Questions: *Where does the President of the United States live and work?*

When did the American Civil War end?

Divide the class into two teams (Team A and Team B). Team A asks Team B the first question. Team B can consult before answering. Then Team B asks Team A the second question, and so on with the other six questions. Score 1 point per correct answer. At the end, the team with the most points is the winner.

ANSWERS:				
	1.	In The White House.	5.	George Washington
	2.	Alaska	6.	Declaration of Independence
	3.	50 States	7.	Los Angeles
	4.	1865	8.	Baseball

UK QUIZ

Question Words + Present Tense Questions:

Where does the Queen live in London?

Ask the two teams to write eight similar questions about Britain (or any other country they know reasonably well). Each question should begin with a different question word. (Some students may need a list of question words written on the board to help them.) Check that the questions are not too difficult and that the team that is to ask the question knows the answer. Also make sure that there is no duplication of questions. The teams then take it in turns to ask the other team a question. Score 1 point per grammatically correct question; 1 point per factually correct answer. At the end, the team with the most points is the winner.

Example questions: (Adapt to the knowledge of your class.)

Where does the Queen live in London?

> *In Buckingham Palace.*

Which city in Scotland is famous for its Arts Festival?

> *Edinburgh.*

How many people live in Britain — to the nearest 5 million?

> *55 million.*

Who is the British Prime Minister?

Why do the British call the 26th of December 'Boxing Day'?

> *It's the day people traditionally give a Christmas box (gift) to tradesmen who call during the year — milkman, postman, etc.*

In which city is Soho?

> *London.*

What colour are the post boxes in Britain?

> *Red.*

USA QUIZ ?

Answer these questions about the United States of America.

Put a ✓ next to the correct answer.

---

1. Where does the President of the USA live and work?

In Congress ☐   In The White House ☐   In The Pentagon ☐

---

2. Which is the biggest state in the USA?

 Texas ☐    California ☐   Alaska ☐

---

3. How many states are there in the USA?

 ☐   ☐    ☐

---

4. When did the American Civil War end?

   1789 ☐   1865 ☐   1776 ☐

---

5. Who was the first president of the USA?

 George Washington ☐   Abraham Lincoln ☐   Ulysses Grant ☐

---

6. Why do the Americans celebrate the 4th of July?

 The first moon landing ☐   Declaration of Independence ☐   The end of the American Civil War ☐

---

7. In which city is Hollywood?

 New York ☐   San Francisco ☐   Los Angeles ☐

---

8. Which is the most popular sport in the USA?

 Baseball ☐    American Football ☐    Tennis ☐

CONNECTIONS 3

Questions: *Can you pass me a knife? – Yes, of course. Here you are.*
Responses: *Have you got a light? – Yes, I have. Here you are. Are you hungry? – No, I'm not.*

Divide the class into small teams of two to three players and appoint team secretaries. Set a four minute time limit for the team secretaries, helped by the rest of their team, to match the questions to the responses. The team with the most correct sentences is the winner.

Hints: Practise the questions and responses afterwards by getting students to ask and answer the questions.

ANSWERS:	A3	B6	C7	D2	E9	F4	G8	H1	I5

QUESTION BAG

Questions, Short answers: *Can you play chess? Have you got a computer? Are you tired?*

Write a number of yes/no question prompts on the board, for example:

> *Can you ...?*
> *Have you got ...?*
> *Are you ...?*
> *Do you like ...?*
> *Would you like ...?*
> *Were you ...?*
> *Did you ... yesterday?*

Practice short answers : *Yes, I can./No, I can't*; *Yes, I have./No, I haven't*, etc. with the class

Get the students to write one question for each prompt on a slip of paper. Explain that the questions should be ones they would like to ask their fellow students (for example, *Can you play chess? Have you got a computer? Are you tired?* etc.). Put the slips of paper into a bag and pass it around the room getting individual students to draw out a question to ask the student sitting next to them. You could award points every time a student answers the questions with the correct short answer form.

CONNECTIONS 3

Connect the question with the answer.

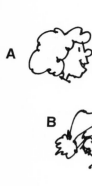 A — CAN YOU PASS ME A KNIFE?

1 YES, I DID.

B — HAVE YOU GOT A LIGHT?

2 I'M HAVING A SHOWER.

C — ARE YOU HUNGRY?

3 YES, OF COURSE. HERE YOU ARE.

D — WHAT ARE YOU DOING?

4 YES, I DO.

E — HOW ARE YOU?

5 OH, YES PLEASE.

F — DO YOU LIKE CLASSICAL MUSIC?

6 YES, I HAVE. HERE YOU ARE.

G — WOULD YOU LIKE A SWEET?

7 NO, I'M NOT.

H — DID YOU SLEEP WELL?

8 NO, THANK YOU.

I — SHALL I ANSWER THE PHONE?

9 I'M VERY WELL, THANK YOU.

A — 3

....

....

....

....

....

MEMORY 5

There was/were: *There was a video recorder under the television.*

Prepositions of place: *There were some paintings on the wall.*

Photocopy pages 77 and 95 to play this game.

Divide the class into small teams of two to three players and appoint team secretaries. Hand out page 77 and give the teams two minutes to study the picture. Then get the teams to cover or hand you back page 77. Hand out page 95 and go through the examples with the class. Make sure the students understand the use of *There was/were.* The team secretaries, helped by the rest of their team, should then write down what things are missing after the burglary. The team with the most correct sentences is the winner. Alternatively, score 2 points if the sentences are both grammatically and factually correct, 1 point if only factually correct. The team with the most points is the winner.

ANSWERS:	1.	There was a video recorder under the television.
	2.	There were some paintings on the wall.
	3.	There were some watches in the drawer of the small desk.
	4.	There was a portable computer on the desk.
	5.	There was a video camera on the shelf.
	6.	There were some glasses in the wall display cabinet.
	7.	There was a handbag on the chair.
	8.	There was a briefcase under the chair.
	9.	There was a vase on top of the cabinet.
	10.	There was a guitar behind the door.

MEMORY 5 – extension

There was/were: *There was a piece of paper next to the dictionary.*

Prepositions of place: *There were two pencils on top of the magazine.*

Place a large number of objects on a desk at the front of the class. Place the objects in such a way that a variety of prepositions of place can be practised, e.g., a piece of paper *next to* a dictionary; two pencils *on top of* a magazine; some coins *near* the cassette recorder; a ruler *inside* a bag; a newspaper *under* a book, etc. You could get the students to help you do this. Then explain that a student should take away and place out of sight five of the objects on the desk while you turn away from the desk. Then turn back to the desk and try to remember where the missing objects were placed. For example:

> You: *There was a piece of paper next to the dictionary.*
> *There were two pencils on top of the magazine.*

Put the missing objects back onto the desk and make some changes in the positioning of the objects. Then get individual students to turn away from the desk while five objects are removed and then try to remember where the objects were. You could award points out of five for this.

Hints: With a large class, this game could be played in small groups of four or five players.

MEMORY 5

1. Look at the things in this room for two minutes. Try to memorise all the things in the room and where they are.

2. Turn the page over.

3. Look at the second page.

NOW ANSWER THE QUESTIONS ON THE SECOND PAGE.

Use these words:

cup   wallet   computer   coat   clock   statue

handbag   camera   book   telephone   guitar   walkman   painting   video recorder

glass

suitcase   video camera   briefcase   bowl   stereo

plate   photograph   vase   watch   television   lamp   violin

77

INSTRUCTIONS QUIZ

Imperative: *First fill the kettle with water.*

Divide the class into small teams of two to three players and appoint team secretaries. The first team to successfully re-arrange pictures A–H and I–P in the correct order and write the instructions is the winner.

Hints: You could also get the players to write their own jumbled up sequences of instructions for the others to solve, for example:

> How to start a car
> look in the mirror, press the accelerator, switch on the ignition, put it in first gear, take off the hand-brake, drive away, press the clutch.

In re-arranging the instructions, the players should use sequence words (*first, next, then* and *finally*).Other ideas for subjects: *How to bath a baby; How to make a telephone call from a call-box; How to clean your teeth.*

ANSWERS:		
	How to make a cup of tea:	*How to make an omelette:*
	First, fill the kettle with water (E).	First, break three eggs into a bowl (K).
	Then boil the water (G).	Then beat the eggs (L).
	Next, warm the teapot (F).	Then season with salt and pepper (M).
	Then put some tea into the teapot (D).	Next, pour a little oil into the pan (O).
	Next, fill the teapot with boiling water (H).	Then heat the oil (I).
	Then leave for a few minutes (B).	Next, pour the mixture into the pan (J).
	Then pour the milk into the cup (A).	Then cook the omelette (N).
	Finally, pour the tea into the cup (C).	Finally, fold the omelette (P).

PLEASE SAY 'PLEASE'

Imperative: *Stand up, please. Don't stand up.*

Ask the class to give you instructions to carry out. Either follow their instructions (if they say *please*), or ignore them (if they don't say *please*). For example:

Player:	*Stand up, please.* (You stand up.)
Player:	*Sit down.* (You remain standing.)
Player:	*Don't stand up.* (You remain standing.)
Player:	*Don't stand up, please.* (You sit down.)
Player:	*Open the window, please.* (You open the window.)

Afterwards, ask the class if they can explain why you sometimes obeyed and sometimes disobeyed their instructions.Then explain that you are going to give them instructions which they have to follow if you say *please* and ignore when you omit *please*. Any player who makes a mistake will get a minus point. Begin to give instructions such as these:

> *Stand up; Smile, please; Don't smile; Don't smile, please.*

The player with the least number of minus points at the end of the game is the winner.
Hints: Play a trial round before playing properly.
You could then play another game with the winner giving instructions to the rest of the class.

INSTRUCTIONS QUIZ

Put these pictures into the correct order and write the instructions.

HOW TO MAKE A CUP OF TEA

A — .... the milk into the cup

B — .... for a few minutes

C — .... the tea into the cup

D — .... some tea into the teapot

E — .... the kettle with water

F — ... the teapot

G — ...the water

H — .... the teapot with boiling water

Use these verbs:	warm		pour	
fill	boil	leave		put

HOW TO MAKE AN OMELETTE

I — .... the oil

J — .... the mixture into the pan

K — .... three eggs into a bowl

L — .... the eggs

M — ....with salt and pepper

N — ... the omelette

O — .... a little oil into the pan

P — ....the omelette

Use these verbs:		pour	heat	
break	season	beat	fold	cook

First fill the kettle with water (E).
Then boil the water (G).
Then...

CATEGORIES 3

Prepositions of Time + Time Words: *In March. On Saturday. At 4 o'clock.*

Working individually (or in pairs), the players write the various time words and expressions under the appropriate column. The first player to categorise the words correctly is the winner.

ANSWERS:	**In**	March	**On**	Saturday	**At**	4 o'clock
		1914		Monday		Christmas
		Autumn		March 1st		midnight
		September		Tuesday morning		half past six
		two minutes		Wednesday evening		a quarter past twelve
		the morning		Friday		2.30

VOTING GAME

Prepositions of Time/ Time Words: *In April. At night. On Wednesday.*

Ask each player to write in large letters the prepositions *in, on* and *at*, separately, on three sheets of paper. While they are doing this, prepare a list of time words and expressions. Explain that you are going to call out a number of time words and expressions and that after each one, the players should 'vote' which is the appropriate preposition of time by holding up the correct sheet of paper. They should 'vote' in unison and not look what the others are doing before deciding. Players get a minus point if they *(a)* hold up the wrong preposition; or *(b)* hesitate too long. Begin to read out your list of time words and expressions, pausing after each one for the players to 'vote' on which preposition to use. Example time words and expressions: *April, night, Wednesday, 1941, May 1st, Monday afternoon, noon, five past six, Easter, half an hour, Spring, my birthday, 6.30.* The player with the least number of minus points at the end of the game is the winner.

Hints: Play a trial round before starting properly.

FOLLOW ON

Days of the Week: *Monday*
Seasons: *Summer*

Begin by saying *Monday*. Explain that the first player has to say the following day *Tuesday*, and then say a different day or season for the next player to follow on. For example:

Player 1:	*Tuesday, Summer.*
Player 2:	*Autumn, Friday.*
Player 3:	*Saturday, Tuesday ...*

The game continues in this way, like a chain drill, round the class. Players get a minus point if they *(a)* don't know the answer; *(b)* make a mistake; or *(c)* hesitate too long. The player with the least number of minus points at the end of the game is the winner.

ADD ON

Time: *5 o'clock*

Begin by saying *five o'clock plus fifteen minutes*. Write this up and explain that the first player has to say the new time (*5 o'clock + 15 minutes = A quarter past five*) and then add on some more time for the next player to work out. For example:

Player 1:	*A quarter past five plus thirty minutes*
Player 2:	*A quarter to six plus five minutes.*
Player 3:	*Ten to six plus ten minutes ...*

The game continues in this way, like a chain drill, round the class. Players get minus points if they *(a)* don't know the answer; *(b)* make a mistake; or *(c)* hesitate too long. The player with the least number of minus points at the end of the game is the winner.

CATEGORIES 3

Time

Look at these time words.
Some use **in**, some use **on**, and some use **at**.

For example:

I'm leaving
in *March.*
on *Saturday.*
at *4 o'clock.*

Put them in the correct column.

March	Saturday	1914	half past six	Wednesday evening	4 o'clock
Monday					2.30
	midnight	a quarter past twelve		two minutes	March 1st
Friday			Autumn		
	the morning	Christmas		Tuesday morning	September

in	on	at
March	*Saturday*	*4 o'clock*

DIRECTIONS GAME

Imperative: *Walk straight on to the end of the road. Then turn right. Take the second turning on the left.*

Prepositions of Movement: *on, down, to*

Divide the class into small teams of two to three players. Introduce the situation and get the teams to work together to complete the task. The team which completes this task correctly in the shortest time is the winner.

Hints: You could then get the teams to write instructions to get to a different place on the map. They could then challenge another team to follow the instructions and find out the name of the place.

ANSWER:	The woman wants to go to the Gate Theatre.

DIRECTIONS GAME – extension

Imperative: *Go out of the room. Turn right and walk to the end of the corridor. Go up the stairs to the next floor.*

Prepositions of Movement: *out of, up, down*

To play this game you will need to work out a set of instructions to direct somebody from the classroom you are in to a room or an area of the building which the students would know, e.g. *the reception, the school library, the toilets, the snack bar*. Explain that you are going to direct somebody to somewhere else in the building and that the class should follow your instructions and say what place you are directing the person to. For example:

You: *Go out of the room. Turn right and walk to the end of the corridor. Go up the stairs to the next floor. Then turn right. Walk along the corridor and it's the third door on the right.*

Then get the students, working in small teams of two or three players, to write instructions directing people to different parts of the building you are working in. They can then challenge the rest of the class to find out which place in the building they are directing somebody to.

Hints: Introduce useful vocabulary like *go up in the lift, first/second/third floor, go down the stairs, walk through the reception, go through the door*.

Directions Game

Where does this woman want to go? Follow the directions on the map and write down the name of the place.

WALK STRAIGHT ON TO THE END OF THE ROAD. THEN TURN RIGHT. TAKE THE SECOND TURNING ON THE LEFT. GO DOWN THE ROAD TILL YOU COME TO A CROSSROADS. TURN RIGHT. THEN TURN RIGHT AGAIN AT THE TRAFFIC LIGHTS. GO DOWN THE ROAD UNTIL YOU COME TO A PARK. THEN TURN LEFT. KEEP STRAIGHT ON FOR ABOUT TWO HUNDRED METRES AND IT'S ON YOUR RIGHT.

She wants to go to ....

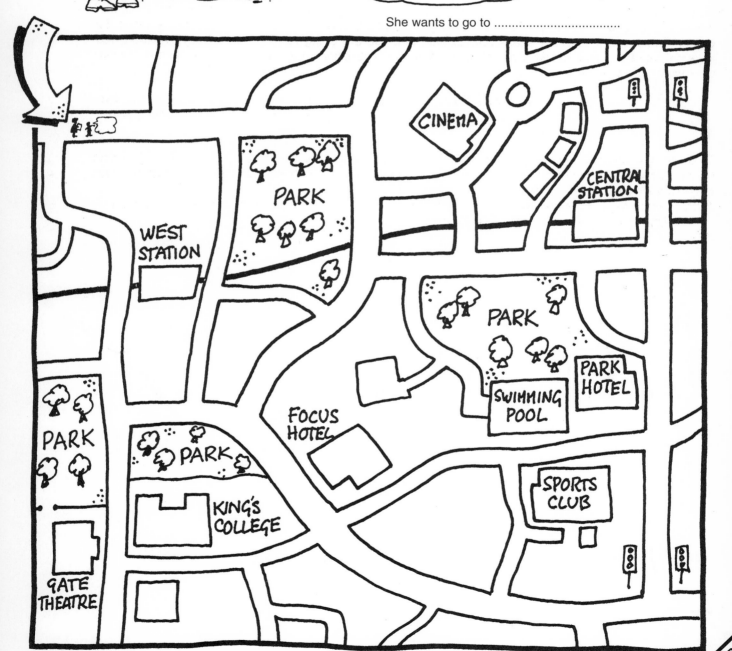

SPELLING QUIZ

Working individually or in pairs, get the students to write answers for the three parts of the quiz. Set an eight minute time limit for them to do this. The player or team with the most correct answers is the winner.

ANSWERS:	**Plural nouns**	**Verb + *ing***	**-*er/-est***
	1. glass/glasses	1. reading	1. happier
	2. box/boxes	2. writing	2. hotter
	3. sandwich/sandwiches	3. sitting	3. shorter
	4. city/cities	4. listening	4. bigger
	5. dish/dishes	5. playing	5. slower
	6. child/children	6. flying	6. later
	7. envelope/envelopes	7. going	7. easier
	8. knife/knives	8. beginning	8. thinner
	9. tomato/tomatoes		
	10. woman/women		

SPELLING QUIZ – extension

Extend the three sections of the spelling quiz with more words. For example:

Plural nouns: church (churches), suitcase (suitcases), bus (buses), fax (faxes), potato (potatoes), radio (radios), baby (babies), factory (factories), mouse (mice), leaf (leaves).

You could present these words with board drawings.

-ing: dance (dancing), ski (skiing), see (seeing), study (studying), die (dying), stop (stopping), hit (hitting), open (opening), cancel (cancelling), plan (planning).

You could get the students to write the *-ing* version of each verb in an example sentence, e.g., *I like dancing.*

-er/-est: cheap (cheaper/cheapest), wide (wider/widest), funny (funnier/ funniest), big (bigger/biggest), busy (busier/busiest), high (higher/highest), fat (fatter/fattest), quick (quicker/quickest), dry (drier/driest).

You could get the students to write the comparative or superlative version of each adjective in an example sentence, e.g., *Which is the cheapest?*

PLURAL NOUNS

Write the plural form of the nouns.

watch *watches*

1.

2.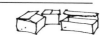

3.

4. o LONDON   o BIRMINGHAM
   o BRISTOL o PARIS

5.

6.

7.

8.

9.

10.

---

child	envelope	knife
watch	tomato	dish
	city	sandwich
glass	box	woman

VERB + -ING

Write the -ing form of the verbs.

She's *having* a bath.

1.

He's .... a magazine.

2.

She's .... a letter.

3.

She's .... on a chair.

4.

He's .... to some music.

5.

She's .... chess.

6.

He's .... by plane.

7.

She's .... to bed.

8.

It's .... to rain.

---

listen	travel	have
read	go	begin
write	play	sit

-ER/-EST

Write the comparative form of the adjectives.

Yours is *larger* than mine.

1.

I'm .... than last year.

2.

It's .... than yesterday.

3.

You're .... than me.

4.

I'd like a .... one.

5.

My car is .... than yours.

6.

I'm sure it's .... than 10.30.

7.

It's .... through here.

8.

You are much .... than last year.

---

short	large	hot
easy	big	slow
late	thin	happy

85

WORD ORDER GAME

Word Order: present and past tense questions and statements; prepositions of time and place; adverbs of time and place; *there is/there are*

Divide the class into small teams of two or three players and appoint team secretaries. The team secretaries, helped by the rest of their team, write the eight sentences in a four-minute time limit. The team with the most correct sentences is the winner.

ANSWERS:	1.	It was very cold yesterday. *or* Yesterday it was very cold.
	2.	They are playing chess in the living room.
	3.	She studies mathematics at university.
	4.	What kind of music do you like?
	5.	There are not any glasses on the table.
	6.	Is there any milk in the fridge?
	7.	I have not got any money.
	8.	I'm going to play tennis this weekend. *or* This weekend, I'm going to play tennis.
	9.	Did you watch TV/television at home last night?

WORD ORDER GAME – extension

Word Order

Working in small teams of two to three players, get the students to agree and write out a fairly complex sentence of between eight and twelve words long. Go round the class checking that the sentences are correctly written as they do this. Then get the teams to rewrite their sentence, writing each word on a separate piece of paper. If their sentence is a question, they should not forget to write a question mark on a separate piece of paper too. Each team then hands the pieces of paper containing their sentence - in jumbled order - to another team to arrange into a sentence. Award points connected to how many seconds the teams take to complete the sentences. For example: *Team A - 45* (seconds); *Team B - 37* (seconds); etc. The teams could then play further rounds. At the end the team with the lowest total of points is the winner.

THE WORD ORDER GAME

You have four minutes to write eight sentences.

1. VERY   YESTERDAY   WAS   IT

It was very cold yesterday or, yesterday it was very cold.

2. LIVING ROOM   ARE   IN   THEY   THE   PLAYING

3. AT   STUDIES $\sqrt{x}(y+z) = a(bc)$ SHE   UNIVERSITY

4. LIKE   OF   WHAT      ?   YOU   DO   KIND

5.    ANY   THE   ON   ARE   THERE   NOT

6. THE   ?   ANY   IS   THERE   IN

7. GOT   HAVE   ANY   I   NOT

8. THIS   TO   I'M   WEEKEND   PLAY   GOING

9. WATCH   AT   NIGHT   ?   YOU   LAST   HOME   DID

87

VERB QUIZ

Present Simple: *You write with a pencil.*

Divide the class into small teams of two to three players and appoint team secretaries. The team secretaries, helped by the rest of their team, write down a sentence for each picture. The first team to do this correctly is the winner.

ANSWERS:	1.	You write with a pen, a pencil and chalk.	

ANSWERS:
1. You write with a pen, a pencil and chalk.
2. You switch on the light, the television and a machine.
3. You eat fruit, meat and vegetables.
4. You read a magazine, a novel and a story.
5. You drive a lorry, a bus and a van.
6. You drink tea, coffee and milk.
7. You carry a briefcase, a suitcase and a handbag.
8. You play table tennis, chess and games.
9. You knit a scarf, gloves and a pullover.
10. You sit on a chair, a stool, and a settee.
11. You live in a bungalow, a house, and a flat.

VERB QUIZ – extension   Verb Forms – Revision

Divide the class into two teams (Team A and Team B). Appoint team secretaries. Write up three circles similar to these:

Team A sets a problem for Team B by choosing one word (or phrase) from each circle. For example: *he, have, yesterday*. Team B's secretary, helped by the rest of the team, then has to write three sentences — a question, a positive statement and a negative statement — based on these three words. For example:

Team B: *Did he have an examination yesterday?*
           He had an examination yesterday.
           He didn't have an examination yesterday.

Score 1 point for each correct sentence. Team B then sets a problem for Team A by choosing a different combination of words (again one from each circle). And so on. At the end, the team with the most points is the winner.

Hints: Help the teams by telling them what verb forms are best to use with each time word or expression. For example:

usually	(Present Simple or Past Simple)
every day	(Present Simple)
just	(Present Perfect)
at the moment	(Present Continuous)
yesterday	(Past Simple)
tomorrow	(Present Continuous — Future use or Going to Future)

VERBING   Verb Forms – Revision

Write a verb on a slip of paper making sure that nobody sees what you write. For example, write *drive*. The class then tries to guess what verb you have written by asking you questions. Write up some sample questions and get the players to start off by asking you those. For example:

Player:	*Am I verbing now?*	You:	*No, you're not.*
Player:	*Do I verb every day?*	You:	*No, you don't.*
Player:	*Did you verb yesterday?*	You:	*Yes, I did.*
Player:	*Can I verb?*	You:	*No, I don't think you can.*
Player:	*Do you verb every day?*	You:	*Yes, I do.*
Player:	*Have you verbed this morning?*	You:	*Yes, I have.*
Player:	*Are you going to verb this evening?*	You:	*Yes, I am.*

And so on, until somebody guesses what verb it is. Give verbal clues if the class gets stuck. The player who guesses is the verb is the next to think of a verb and be questioned. And so on.

VERB QUIZ

Find three nouns to go with each verb.

1. write with

2. switch on

3. eat

4. read

5. drive

6. drink

7. carry

8. play

9. knit

10. sit on

11. live in

pullover	suitcase	machine	meat	chess	gloves	scarf coffee
milk story		house	van	chalk	magazine	fruit
lorry					games	chair
vegetables		bus	flat	table tennis	bungalow	pencil
handbag	settee	novel	briefcase	television	tea stool	light pen

1. You write with a pen, a pencil and chalk.

2. ....

3. ....

4. ....

5. ....

6. ....

7. ....

8. ....

9. ....

10. ....

11. ....

89

VOCABULARY QUIZ

Vocabulary Revision

Working individually (or in pairs), the players complete the six sections of the vocabulary quiz. Set a ten minute time limit. Score 1 point for each correct answer. The player with the most correct answers is the winner.

ANSWERS:

Opposites	It's a ...	Synonyms
thin/thick	1. A screwdriver	like=enjoy
cheap/expensive	2. A heater	close=shut
love/hate	3. A pillow	answer=reply
large/small	4. A kettle	return=come back
easy/difficult	5. A tap	sick=ill
early/late	6. A fork	tidy=neat
near/far	7. A plug	sad=unhappy
short/long	8. A saucepan	correct=right

Odd Word Out	Spelling	Countries and Nationalities
Colours - dark	OPTICIAN	1. France - French
Animals - beef	SHOWER	2. Russia - Russian
Vegetables - pears	KITCHEN	3. India - Indian
Clothes - feet	HAMMER	4. Egypt - Egyptian
Relatives - boy	SHEEP	5. Kenya - Kenyan
Furniture - window	SPOON	6. Brazil - Brazilian
Jobs - husband	SAUSAGES	7. Canada - Canadian
Materials - strong	LORRY	8. Sweden - Swedish

THE CROSSWORD GAME

Vocabulary Revision

Each player draws a square divided into five squares by five on a piece of paper. (If the class is larger than eight players it is probably better to play in teams of pairs.) Each player in turn calls out any letter of the alphabet. As each letter is called, all players write it into a square of their choice. The aim is to form as many words as possible of two or more letters reading either across or down. Players continue to call out letters until all the individual squares have been filled in. The players then total up the points they have scored. The number of points scored is equal to the number of letters in each word they have made. Thus a three-letter word scores 3 points. One-letter words do not count. Letters cannot be used twice in the same direction; for example the same *p* cannot be used twice to make *pop* and *pot*. Long words could be rewarded by giving a bonus point for five-letter words. The player with the highest score is the winner.

Hints: Play a trial game on the board with one student to illustrate how the game is played before playing properly. Before playing, tell the players *(a)* once a letter has been written down it cannot be moved to another square; and *(b)* no abbreviations or proper nouns are allowed.

Go round the class as the game is being played to check that everybody understands what to do.

CHANGE A LETTER

Vocabulary Revision

Begin by saying *play*. Explain that the first player has to make a new word out of *play* by changing one letter. For example, he or she could say *plan*. The next player then has to make a new word out of *plan* by again changing one letter, e.g. *flan*. The game continues with each player in turn trying to make a new word out of the word he or she has been given. Players get a minus point if they *(a)* can't think of a new word; or *(b)* hesitate too long. Example round with a group of five players:

Player 1:	*Plan.*
Player 2:	*Flan.*
Player 3:	*Flat.*
Player 4:	... (This player can't think of a new word and so gets a minus point.)
Player 5:	(This player starts with a new word.) *Make.*
Player 1:	*Take.*

And so on. The player with the least number of minus points at the end of the game is the winner.

Hints: Play a trial round before playing properly. It is probably best to stick to words of three or four letters at this level.

Vocabulary Quiz

OPPOSITES

expensive thick
near
early short
easy
cheap
love
thin
small
large
far difficult
late
long hate

thin/thick

SPELLING

OPTICIAN

SYNONYMS

like   answer   sick   sad   come back
ill
shut   close   return   tidy   correct
neat   right   enjoy
reply   unhappy

like = enjoy

IT'S A...

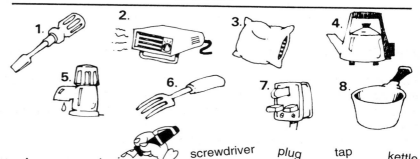

1. 2. 3. 4.
5. 6. 7. 8.

1. A screwdriver

screwdriver   plug   tap   kettle
saucepan   pillow   heater   fork

ODD WORD OUT

Colours
yellow
dark ✗
green
orange
pink

Animals
pig
horse
cow
beef
cat

Vegetables
cabbage
potatoes
pears
beans
peas

Clothes
jacket
feet
socks
skirt
shirt

Relatives
boy
son
sister
parents
daughter

Furniture
bed
chair
settee
desk
window

Jobs
waiter
doctor
actor
clerk
husband

Materials
steel
wool
plastic
strong
wood

COUNTRIES AND NATIONALITIES

1. PARIS
2. MOSCOW
3. DELHI
4. CAIRO
5. NAIROBI
6. BRASILIA
7. OTTAWA
8. STOCKHOLM

1. France - French

MEMORY 3

What presents have these people got?

Can you remember?

1. ....He's got a pair of trainers.....

2. ....They've got some glasses.....

3. ....

4. ....

5. ....

6. ....

7. ....

Answer these questions about the picture.

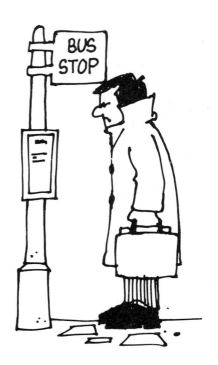

1. Did he make the bed? ..... *No, he didn't.* .....
2. Did he have breakfast? ..... *Yes, he did.* .....
3. Did he have coffee for breakfast? .....
4. Did he have an egg? .....
5. Did he close the window? .....
6. Did he open his mail? .....
7. Did he read the morning newspaper? .....
8. Did he wash up the dishes? .....
9. Did he take his umbrella to work? .....
10. Did he have a shower this morning? .....
11. Did he do any washing? .....
12. Did he switch off the gas? .....
13. Did he switch off the light in the bedroom? .....
14. Did he make the bed? .....

Write what things are missing from the room after the burglary. Do not look at the first page again until you have finished.

1. There was a video recorder under the television.
2. There were some paintings on the wall.
3.
4.
5.
6.
7.
8.
9.
10.

95

INDEX OF STRUCTURE AND LANGUAGE POINTS